Praise for *Trouble, Triumph, and Truth*

Donna Wilcox's life is an interesting story! It is a saga of events that will inspire and encourage each one of us in our spiritual journey. *Trouble, Triumph, and Truth* is a fascinating and refreshing read which will challenge you the next time you're confronted with a situation that appears helpless and out of control. Proverbs 24:10 (*The Message*) says, "If you fall to pieces in a crisis, there wasn't much to you in the first place." There is much to Donna! As her pastor I have witnessed firsthand her *Trouble, Triumph, and Truth*. Bolt in!

Pastor Randy Popineau
Church at Briargate
Colorado Springs, Colorado

As Director of ACTS Ministries at The Harbor Assembly of God Church in Navarre, Florida, I feel truly blessed to have known Donna Wilcox for more than ten years. In those years, I have experienced first hand her undying dedication to many different positions to include: choir director, world missions director, women's ministry and motivational speaker, author, missionary, teacher, counselor, intercessor, mentor, and personal beloved friend. You will not find anyone more genuine and sincere than Donna. If this devotional is anything in comparison to her first book *Falling into Faith,* hold on to your seat. You will experience truth, passion for the Word of God, and laughter; all wrapped up in one package under the anointed teaching and writing of Donna Wilcox.

Sherrie D. Johnson
Director, ACTS Ministries
Holley-Navarre, Florida

Donna Wilcox embodies the true meaning of character in every sense of the word. She sets a wonderful example for all of us on how to really "live" life. As a person who has sometimes struggled with faith, I can say that Donna has truly shown me its power. If only all of us could be as impervious to opposition and negativity. In whatever form you receive Donna's words of wisdom, heed them as they are truth delivered with true conviction and by a real example.

Julie Gentry
Director of High School Admissions
CollegeAmerica, Stevens-Henager College, and California College of
    San Diego
And Friend

Donna's zest for life and love of God's Word is an inspiration! As you read this devotional, and the words of God wash over you, you will be moved to a place of true worship. Donnas' complete obedience and utter faith in the Lord will encourage and lift you up. Get ready for a great ride!

Shelley Richards
Regional Director
International Bible Society
A Global Affiliate of IBS-STL

The minute I met Donna, I felt like I'd known her for years. Her warmth, exuberance and fire for Jesus is catching and exhilarating. She is always ready to proclaim the word, in season and out of season. Her first book, *Falling into Faith*, was compelling, transparent and hard to put down. Donna's new book, *Trouble, Triumph, and Truth*, will encourage you through true stories and devotionals that coincide with them. I know you will be blessed.

Teresa Marshall
Christian Ministry Product Administrator
Colorado Springs, Colorado

Trouble, Triumph, and Truth

A Devotional with Lessons from Life That
Will Powerfully Transform Your Thinking!

Dr. Donna Wilcox

PublishAmerica

Hardcover 9781448916610
Softcover 9781606104446
PUBLISHED BY PUBLISHAMERICA, LLLP
www.publishamerica.com

"But we have this treasure in jars of clay to show that this all-surpassing power is from God and not from us. *We are hard pressed on every side, but not crushed; perplexed, but not in despair; persecuted, but not abandoned; struck down, but not destroyed.*"
(2 Corinthians 4:7-9, NIV, emphasis added)

Scripture Quotations Taken From:

Introduction

Throughout the pages of my autobiography *Falling into Faith,* you read about my life and the miraculous healings I experienced. I detailed the amazing transformation that happened throughout the years, as God brought forth beauty and blessings from years of pain and despair. You also gained an understanding of the importance of a growing faith. A faith that learns to continuously choose to *fall* into a trust relationship with a loving and faithful Father; even when life throws you a curve, and you do not understand how in the world anything good can come of it! I pray it encouraged your heart to lean upon Jesus Christ in a greater way and enriched your love walk between God and man.

Trouble, Triumph, and Truth has truly been a labor of love, and I pray your heart is greatly encouraged as you read this devotional. Each chapter is an inspirational and unique devotion that deals with real-life issues. Using a compilation of true stories from not only my life, but friends and family as well; it teaches Biblical truths and Godly wisdom on how to victoriously press through the challenges we face in this life. I believe each chapter will edify your spirit and touch your heart in a profound way.

Falling in love with Jesus Christ and choosing to serve Him are the best things that can ever happen to anyone. He does amazingly more than we dare to dream or imagine! Never stop growing in your walk with Christ. Saturate your life with His Word and walk in obedience. A bountiful harvest of blessings awaits those who refuse to settle for mediocrity and chooses to press into God. Regardless of the circumstances or impossibilities, a powerful peace and contagious joy will consume you like a warm blanket on a cold winter's night as you strive, stand, and grow in God.

You may ask, "How is this possible?" The answer is simple; *it is Jesus.* He alone has the power to completely heal and restore. One important step toward healing in every area of life is the restoration of joy and laughter to our mind, body, and spirit. The Bible tells us, "The joy of the Lord is our strength," and you will discover the power of *joy* through many of the stories and life lessons throughout this devotional.

Another important step is to practice a lifestyle of giving. We must have the heart of a servant, and a servant-driven life. How do we accomplish this necessary task? We must unselfishly give of ourselves in service to others and give to things that have eternal value. Throughout the following pages I discuss numerous ways we can all make a difference, and the enormous benefits that continuously flows through the lives of those who embrace this principle.

In this devotional I refer to Jesus Christ, God the Father, and the Holy Spirit. God is a single being existing simultaneously as three distinct persons. The Bible clearly speaks of God the Father, God the Son (Jesus Christ) and God the Holy Spirit. According to scripture, the three are co-equal and co-eternal, one in essence, nature, power, action, and will.

So, get ready to have fun and laugh aloud when you read about the trouble. Prepare to rejoice when you experience the triumph. Finally, may your heart overflow with unashamed praise to the King of kings, the Lord of lords, and Redeemer of our lives as you read about His truth! I pray you find the Bible lessons unique and enjoyable, *but don't keep it to yourself; make a point to share the Good News with others.*

"Faith never knows where it is being led, but it loves and knows the One who is leading."
—Oswald Chamber

Dedication

First and foremost, with heartfelt gratitude I want to praise to my Heavenly Father for His unconditional mercy and love. It is a privilege to serve my Lord and Savior Jesus Christ.

To my loving husband Bob, thank you for your faithful love and support. The truth is, every blonde should have a Bob. I love you, baby!

To Mom and Dad, I love and miss you. Thank you for always being there for me with prayer, love, and encouragement.

To my beautiful stepdaughter Traci, thank you for allowing me to be a part of your life. I pray your nursing career is filled with many opportunities to be an extension of Christ.

A big thank you and I love you from *Mama Donna* to all of our God-given sons, daughters, and grand-children. You are truly loved and we are grateful for each and every one of you. Thank you most of all for allowing me to experience the joy of motherhood. Being *Mama Donna* is the role in life I cherish the most. Bob and I feel blessed to be a part of your lives. The last count was forty-nine…Amazing! We truly are a great *BIG,* happy family.

Thank you to everyone who submitted a story. Your testimonies touched my heart and increased my faith. I pray many will be blessed and encouraged. Friends and Family are a precious gift and I treasure each one of you!

Thank you to everyone who purchased my autobiography, *Falling into Faith.* I am honored and humbled by your generosity and the many kind e-mails and correspondences I continue to receive expressing how my testimony has touched your lives.

Special thanks to my cousin Gloria Grant Bailey and her wonderful husband Anthony. You were always there to lend a helping hand with

Dad, (and everyone else in the family). You are our rock, and we love you!

Thank you Paul and Jackie Roberts for your love and friendship. Throughout the years you have been steadfast, faithful, and true friends to our entire family. We love you!

Thank you to my cousin David Grant, His wife Beth, and their two beautiful daughters, Jennifer and Rebecca. I cannot express the appreciation I feel in my heart for your work in India and other countries over the years. You have rescued so many from a life of pain and despair. As you continue to help those who are victims of human trafficking, may God do abundantly more than you dare to dream or imagine. Stay the course and keep the faith…I love you!

Thank you to all the wonderful Christian organizations who are focused on getting God's Word translated into every language and placed in the hands of every human being. May the windows of Heaven open up and abundantly bless and revolutionize your efforts!

Bob and Donna Wilcox

Rev. Edward and Mary Grant

Foreword

If you had the fortune of reading Donna's autobiography, *Falling into Faith,* you are familiar with the struggles that have molded her into one of the most incredible people that I have had the privilege to know. Donna is passionate in every area of her life. She is the friend that you yearn for and the dedicated employee that CEOs around the country spend years searching to find. She makes the workplace fun and exciting just by coming to work.

Donna is also on fire for Jesus. She shows it in her daily walk, with all of the "kids" that she is "Mom" to in the workplace and home, as well as the volunteer work she does in the community.

Matthew 5:14-16 (NIV) states: "You are the light of the world. A city on a hill cannot be hidden. Neither do people light a lamp and put it under a bowl. Instead they put it on its stand, and it gives light to everyone in the house. In the same way, let your light shine before men, that they may see your good deeds and praise your Father in heaven."

Donna is that light to everyone she encounters, and as you read this book she will be a light to you.

—Rozann Kunstle
CollegeAmerica Campus President
Colorado Springs, Colorado

Contents

Chapter 1

Bats, Brooms, and Strainers .

"A cheerful heart is good medicine." (Proverbs 17:22, NIV)

Scripture Focus

"For ye shall go out with joy, and be led forth with peace: the mountains and the hills shall break forth before you into singing, and all the trees of the field shall clap their hands." (Isaiah 55:12, KJV)

"I will greatly rejoice in the Lord, my soul shall be joyful in my God; for He hath clothed me with the garments of salvation, He hath covered me with the robe of righteousness, as a bridegroom decketh himself in ornaments, and as a bride adorneth herself with her jewels." (Isaiah 61:10, KJV)

"You have turned my mourning into joyful dancing. You have taken away my clothes of mourning and clothed me with joy, that I might sing praises to You and not be silent. O Lord my God, I will give you thanks forever." (Psalm 30:11, 12, NLT)

A True Story from the Life of Bob and Donna Wilcox

By Dr. Donna Wilcox

For several years, Bob and I lived in the middle of the Sangre de Cristo Mountains and worked as Pastoral Missionaries at a Mission's Training School. We were so far from civilization cell phones rarely worked, and to get to the nearest town meant driving quite a distance through winding mountainous roads. I use the word "town" loosely; however, it did have a Wal-Mart!

City living is usually cluttered with hustle and bustle, among other things that distract and annoy; but living in the mountains proved to be peaceful, slow, and easy. We could jump on our four-wheeler and drive all over the mountain soaking in the beautiful view of God's creation, then pick a spot and spend time just talking with the Father and contemplating life. Those times of sweet communion continue to be a treasured memory.

Our living quarters consisted of a quaint three-bedroom log cabin, always brimming about with numerous activities, and of course, down-home Southern cooking! We cherish those memories along with the continued blessings in our lives from the great big wonderful family God has given us. We spent many nights together in prayer and Bible studies (and debates), as well as times of uncontrollable laughter and playing games into the wee hours of the morning.

Living in the mountains certainly had its advantages, but there were also some disadvantages. Late one night while Bob lay sleeping and I was just about to doze off, I heard a strange, screeching and fluttering sound. Sitting up in bed I wondered, *What in the world can that be?* It was common for bears to break into homes and cabins in the mountains, but this did not sound like a bear. Suddenly, I heard it again. Bouncing out of bed, I ran down the hall to the den just in time to see what looked like a bird flying low across the room. My first thought was, *I shouldn't wake Bob up; he worked hard today. I can probably take care of this; after all, it's only a bird.* Then wisdom kicked in. *Are you kidding? It will end up on your head, and you will start screaming like a little girl. He will wake up thinking someone is trying to kill you!*

Since moving to the mountains Bob had been good at handling the critters and crawly things, so why rob him of this blessing once again! With that in mind, I ran back to the room to wake up my knight in shining armor and brief him on the situation. With a puzzled look he sat up and responded, "Baby, are you sure it's a bird?"

I quickly replied, "What else can it be?" Then I said, "Wait here and I'll go look one more time." So being a brave missionary (ha), I immediately headed off to get a better look at the mysterious flying creature. Knowing it had flown into the kitchen, I boldly turned on a light just in time to realize something terrifying. *That is not a bird. Lord help me; IT'S A BAT!* You see, a bird does not hang upside down and attach itself to the side of a wall.

Running back to the room I gave my man the news, "Baby, it's a bat, go kill it!"

Half-asleep and a little dazed, Bob (a brave man of God and known for strategy and detail) proceeded toward the kitchen quietly deciphering a plan of attack. After a few moments of careful consideration he grabbed a broom, and *BAM!* No more bat. Now, before you get all activist on me, I, too, love creatures big and small and do not like to kill anything, but sometimes you have to draw a line for the sake of sanity!

The next night, we were watching television, and Bob decided to go on to bed. Being the night owl in the family and not ready to go to sleep, I kissed him goodnight and said I would be in shortly. While I sat in my glider watching an old *Matlock* episode, something came out of nowhere and flew across the room. I immediately thought; *Surely this can't be another bat!* Before I could move, it once again swooshed down right over the top of my head. I started to yell for Bob to come to my rescue, but before I could utter a word I felt a sudden jolt of empowerment. In a brave and firm voice I said, "Listen here, bat; there is no way you are going to get the best of me. Prepare for battle!"

I quickly discovered something about bats; they are difficult to catch and oddly cute, (in an ugly kind of way). One more thing preyed on my mind. *I've invested forty-five minutes into this murder mystery and I want to know how it ends; the bat will just have to wait. But what am I going to do about it flying over my head and taunting me?*

Bob had baseball caps, but I needed something sturdy and protective. Then I remembered, *I have a plastic vegetable and pasta strainer in the kitchen. I'll just put that over my head until the show is over, and then I'll run to the bedroom and close the door. Good thinking, Donna!* In case you are wondering, yes, I talk to myself quite often.

The strainer had a long handle, so I turned the handle off to the side to keep my vision from being obscured. So picture it, there I sat, a grown woman watching television with a strainer on my head and a bat swooshing by every few minutes. Too curious for my own good I decided to sneak a peak in the mirror, and let me tell you, when I am having a bad day all I have to do is think about my reflection staring back at me and uncontrollable laughter soon follows. I looked like a rapper with a real strange hat! Bob regrets that we don't have a picture or video of my rapper look, but I cannot say that I agree. It would only provide additional proof that I am slightly wacky!

So, what did I learn? First, God has quite a sense of humor and living in a log cabin in the mountains can be a wild adventure. Second, I am pretty resourceful with kitchen utensils. Third, bats are so ugly they are cute. And finally, Bob is a very good husband who really knows how to use a broom!

~The End~

Truth

Nehemiah 8:10 says, "The joy of the Lord is your strength," and Proverbs 17:22 says, "A cheerful heart is good medicine." If you are having a bad day or feeling spiritually and emotionally weak, seek joy and begin praising God. The joy that comes from the Lord will give you the strength and courage to face the challenges of life. You may even find reflecting on my bat story will bring a smile to your face and some much-needed laughter. You have my permission to laugh *at* or *with me,* whatever helps!

Scripture tells us in 1 Thessalonians 5:16, "be joyful always." This applies to every situation life dishes out, not just when things are wonderful or we feel blissfully happy. Regardless of our circumstances, God is a good Father who deserves our praise and gratitude! 1 Thessalonians 5:18 says, "Give thanks in all circumstances, for this is God's will for you in Christ Jesus." The only way to accomplish this is by obedience to the Word and choosing to step out in faith and become *doers,* not *hearers* only.

How is this possible when we are experiencing pain and disappointment? With the help of the Holy Spirit combined with courage, conviction, and soaking in the Word of God, "We demolish arguments and every pretension that sets itself up against the knowledge of God, and we take captive every thought to make it obedient to Christ." (2 Corinthians 10:5, NIV) In other words, we must choose to *cast down, demolish,* and *utterly destroy* every thought that enters our mind which is contrary to God's Word and His will for our lives. By speaking Biblical truths to our situation, we are putting faith in action and proactively *taking captive every thought and making it obedient to Christ.*

If you have accepted Christ as the Savior of your life, remember something important; whatever pain and difficulty you are facing, our Heavenly Father has equipped you with everything you need to victoriously forge through and overcome your situation. This has not taken Him by surprise. Trust in His Word, His power, and His strength. You are not alone and God is a powerful and limitless Father! His Word promises in our weakness He will be our strength.

It boils down to one thing, *a matter of choice.* When the enemy fills your mind with doubt and confusion, take authority over those thoughts and feelings. In the precious name of Jesus and with unwavering faith, stand upon God's Word.

Below are just a few examples of the enemy's deceptive lies:

- This situation is only going to get worse, and there is no hope
- You heard the doctor's report; things are bad and it is just a matter of time
- My child will never come to Jesus because he/she is too deep in sin
- I will always be in debt and never find a job with good pay and benefits
- There is no hope for my marriage because He/she does not love me anymore

I am not suggesting we should deny the reality of our situation; however, we must learn to give those things over to God, seek His wisdom, and rest in His power. The enemy wants us to believe our lives will never get better and there is no hope to be found; however, the Word says the Father desires to bless His children with good things and a life that is fruitful in every way. These promises are also for our family because the Bible states they are for "our seed" and "from generation to generation."

If problems are mounting and joy seems far away, take a small step forward and apply a time of praise to your day. Take five or ten minutes to think on God's blessings and what His Word says about your life. If a negative thought comes to mind, replace it with His truth. Refuse to allow how you are feeling, your circumstances, or what the facts are screaming at you to dictate your decision to praise Him! Once you have conquered a five or ten-minute interval, next time go for fifteen minutes. Each day continue in praise and thanksgiving. Before you know it, feelings or circumstances will no longer rule and control your life.

In my book *Falling into Faith,* I referred to an old saying that has made an enormous impact on my attitude and prayer life: "Feelings make great servants but terrible masters." If we allow feelings and emotions to dictate our actions and choices, we will never fully understand or grasp what it means to live an overcoming life and walk in victory.

Dwelling on negative circumstances will get us nowhere fast. God is bigger than our problems, more powerful than the enemy will ever be, and able to do so much more than we dare to dream or imagine! Before we can fully realize the impact of God's power in our lives, we must change our thinking habits. This takes a firm commitment; along with consistency, prayer, and determination.

When my mother was battling cancer, she meditated on 2 Corinthians 4:16-18. It gave her strength to face the pain and treatments she endured. Mom possessed a spirit of joy, never losing the ability to laugh and rest in God's peace. She often shared with me how she longed to see Jesus and the excitement she felt knowing a home in Heaven awaited her. I listened as she talked but did not share her enthusiasm. The thought of life without mom felt too painful. It has been a number of years since she went to be with Jesus, and I finally understand what Mom was trying to teach me about life and hardships. I too have discovered a lot of comfort and wisdom found in the words of 2 Corinthians 4:16-18.

"Therefore, *we do not lose heart,* though outwardly we are wasting away, yet inwardly, we are being renewed day by day. For our light and momentary troubles are achieving for us eternal glory that far outweighs them all. So we fix our eyes *not* on what is seen, but on what is unseen, for what is seen is temporary, but what is unseen is eternal." 2 Corinthians 4:16-18 [NIV, emphasis added].

In conclusion, if you are longing for an overcoming and joyful life, the Bible gives precise instructions on how to achieve it. First, daily read and study the Bible. Second, ask the Holy Spirit to open your spiritual eyes and ears to the truth of God's Word. Third, choose right thinking and resist the enemy's lies and clever attempts to keep your focus on the problems or difficulties you are facing. Finally, fall into the powerful arms of God and laugh! Surround yourself with things that bring joy and refuse to allow your feelings to control your existence. Remember, "The joy of the Lord is your strength," and "A cheerful heart is good medicine."

Take time to get alone with God and meditate on the following scriptures, then apply them to every area of your life. Continuously remind yourself of one important fact; nothing is impossible with Jesus Christ our Lord.

Ultimately, the decision to overcome is up to us, because Christ will never force us to let go of our burdens and give them over to Him. Choose well, choose life, and joy will follow!

"Rejoice in the Lord always. I will say it again: Rejoice!" Let your gentleness be evident to all. The Lord is near. *Do not be anxious* about anything, but in everything, by prayer and petition, with thanksgiving, *present your requests to God.* And the peace of God, *which transcends all understanding,* will guard your hearts and your minds in Christ Jesus. Finally, brothers, *whatever is true, whatever is noble, whatever is right, whatever is pure, whatever is lovely, whatever is admirable, if anything is excellent or praiseworthy, think about such things.* Whatever you have learned or received or heard from me, or seen in me, *put it into practice.* And the God of peace *will be with you."* (Philippians 4:4-9, NIV, emphasis added)

Chapter 2

The Disease of Complacency

"Never lag in zeal and in earnest endeavor; be aglow and burning with the Spirit, serving the Lord." (Romans 12:11, AMP)

Scripture Focus

"Woe to you who are complacent in Zion, and to you who feel secure on Mount Samaria…" (Amos 6:1, NIV)

"Wake up! Strengthen what remains and is about to die, for I have not found your deeds complete in the sight of my God. Remember, therefore, what you have received and heard; obey it, and repent. But if you do not wake up, I will come like a thief, and you will not know at what time I will come to you." (Revelation 3:2-3, NIV)

"These are the words of the Amen, the Faithful and True Witness, the Ruler of God's creation. I know your deeds, that you are neither cold nor hot. I wish you were either one or the other!" (Revelation 3:15, NIV)

Faith for Real

By Bethanie Neely

"What fire is in mine ears?"
—Beatrice, in *Much Ado About Nothing*, William Shakespeare

I live in Colorado Springs, the veritable Christian Mecca of the Midwest, and I work at Focus on the Family. I attend church on Wednesdays and Sundays. Every Tuesday morning I have coffee with my father, and we do Bible studies together. Only one of my friends is a non-Christian, and she lives on the other side of the country. Nearly everyone in my life—everyone I spend my time with, everyplace I go, every part of my day—I am influenced by Christianity. I have a fish bumper sticker on my car, Christian T-shirts, and I even have a cross tattoo. Why do I feel so powerless as a Christian?

Everything that surrounds me should remind me of the awesome power of the Lord, but recently I began noticing things have dwindled down in my faith since I came to Christ on July 23, 2000. I asked myself, *Where is the passion? Where is the purpose?* You see, I no longer wrote in my journal every day, or felt drawn as I once was to the Bible. The Word of the Living God did not attract me. There was something seriously wrong.

I know there are those of you who feel this way. John and Stasi Eldredge put it perfectly in their book, *Captivating.* "Walk into any church in America, take a look around, and ask yourself this question, 'What is a Godly woman?' Don't listen to what is said; listen to the lives of the women present. What do we learn? A Godly woman is…tired."

Eldredge's *Wild at Heart* gives us a similar definition for men: "Walk into most churches, have a look around, and ask yourself: 'What is a Christian man?' Without listening to what is said, look at what you find there. Most Christian men are…bored."

So, we have "tired" and "bored." Search your heart. If you think about it long enough, you will realize that this is a very honest reality. It is also a very sad one. When was the last time you felt a true genuine joy in your walk with the Lord? Be honest now; were you drinking anything with caffeine beforehand? Or eating chocolate?

I used to have a Friday morning Mocha Meet with some women from my church. Sometimes we got into Biblical discussions, sometimes we talked about, well, women stuff. Driving to work afterwards, I often felt somewhat joyful. I began to recognize those days by what I ordered from the barista at the coffee house.

I started to realize something; I was seriously suffering in my relationship with the Lord. Sure, I counted on Jesus for my salvation. I tried to do what was right. I attended church and checked the boxes of my faith "to do" list. Yet I felt both tired and bored at the same time.

For two glorious months after my decision for Christ, I wrote in a journal every day. I obsessively read my Bible and prayed all the time. God spoke to me through His Word and through the most amazing dreams. Christian music communicated God's heart to me. I was consistently *pursuing*, so what happened? I got busy. I got distracted. The novelty of being a Christian wore off, and I was faced with the same, uneventful, boring life—a job every day, Church, the same people, the same, same, same. Life should be more exciting for a Christian, shouldn't it?

"I tell you the truth, anyone who has faith in Me will do what I have been doing. He will do even greater things than these, because I am going to the Father." (John 14:12, NIV)

This is not just a nice verse with a quaint blessing, folks. This is the promise of Jesus to His people. Why are we acting as the same people we were before we met Jesus? Why aren't we doing great and amazing things with our faith? If you are doing great things, then you can skip over this; I am simply berating myself here. This is a reminder to me about what a great privilege it is to be a Child of God.

Working at Focus, we have devotionals for about a half hour every morning. This is a time when we get together and pray, or someone reads a passage, and then we all go to our desks and get on with the day. The purpose is to get us in the right frame of mind for the day. It is actually a very good principle, and although it costs the ministry thousands of dollars weekly, it is a good thing!

One morning the person who organized devotionals invited a guest. The man's name was Khodor Shami. He was born and raised a Muslim, and met Jesus Christ in a very real way. On this particular morning, he spoke about being real in our faith. He referenced the parable of the talents, expressing how each of us needs to do what we are called to do for Christ. There was a fire in my ears when he spoke, and I realized as Christians we need to agitate ourselves.

We need to wake up because the Lord is coming back, and many of the people who consider themselves Christians are living the same tired, boring lives. It is not necessarily an advantage to be born and raised in the Christian faith, because it appears we have tried to tame God.

Khodor Shami grew up a Muslim, a faith that taught him to hate the Christian belief. In spite of this, and because of many amazing meetings with Christians who were alive in their faith, he experienced the power of the Living God first hand, and it changed his life!

This is the message we need to be telling people, and I am so thankful Khodor came to speak. It reminded me that every day I should awake with the name of Jesus on my lips. I need to be on my knees as the sun rises and thank the Lord that He has called me for such a time as this.

God has given each of us a passion. Think about it. What is your passion? I bet you can say it aloud without even thinking. What is in your gut to do? Do you wonder how you can serve the Lord as a hairdresser, or a burger-flipper at McDonald's? You can pray. You can claim the ground you step on as the Lord's territory, and you can live your Christianity out!

"Therefore, my dear friends, as you have always obeyed—not only in my presence, but now much more in my absence—continue to work out your salvation with fear and trembling, for it is God who works in you to will and to act according to His good purpose." (Philippians 2:12-13, NIV)

Prayer

This is my cry, Lord Jesus. Help! Show me *Your* purpose for my life today. Send me. I will go, and do not let me live a boring life! Make me *Your* servant, and give me the power to do *Your* work. Do not let me sleep complacently—wake me up. Set my heart on fire. AMEN!

~The End~

Truth

I met Beth when I ministered to the pastoral staff at Focus on the Family. Her energy and passion for Jesus shone through in an honest and sincere way.

After ministering to the staff, I shared my vision for *Trouble, Triumph, and Truth*. I asked if anyone had a story of how God answered prayer concerning a specific issue in their life to please consider submitting it for my book project. Little did I know Beth has a passion for Jesus and writing. She e-mailed a manuscript to me about her life, and when I came to the chapter "Faith for Real" I immediately knew it must be in my devotional, and Beth graciously consented.

Beth's honesty struck a chord in my heart. It is so easy, too easy, to forget the majestic beauty of our Savior and the mercy He extended to all who call on His name. Complacency causes us to take the Lord and His amazing grace for granted as it weaves a dangerous web of laziness, mediocrity, bad attitudes, and so much more.

When you hear the word, "complacent," what comes to mind? The American Heritage Dictionary gives this definition: "Contented to a fault; self-satisfied and unconcerned." Another definition describes it like this: "Smug, unbothered, and untroubled." A Christian should not be any of these things!

The Bible has much to say about complacency and we should pay close attention to the scriptures. If we heed God's Word blessings will flow out of our lives, and more importantly, opportunities to share the love of Christ.

"For the waywardness of the simple will kill them, and the complacency of fools will destroy them; but whoever listens to Me will live in safety and be at ease, without fear of harm." (Proverbs 1:32-33)

Allowing complacency in our lives can also cause Christians to enter into what I call a *spiritual bubble*. This is where we surround ourselves with everything and everyone "Christian." Although we may feel physically and spiritually safe, it is not a lifestyle which lines up with the example Christ gave us. How can we be a light in the world if we do not reach out to those who do not know our wonderful Savior? Shouldn't we follow the example of Christ? When Jesus walked this earth He reached out to the broken and hurting everywhere He went. Who are we to do any different? We must not permit ourselves to be smug, unbothered, or untroubled toward others. Our mission on this earth is to spread the *Good News of Jesus Christ* to those who are lost and hurting, as well as encourage and lift up our brothers and sisters in the Lord. If we shut ourselves off from the world, we have made a conscious decision to refuse our very purpose and mission!

We are **all** sinners saved by grace. Romans 3:23 [NLT] tells us, "For everyone has sinned; we all fall short of God's glorious standard." The words, "everyone" and "all" means no one is exempt, including those of us who are saved! Regardless of how many scriptures we can recite or how many hours a day we spend praying, we will not reach perfection until we get to heaven. While we are on this earth and there is still time, let us make a conscious and purposeful decision to be about our Father's business.

We must understand complacency is far reaching, and the results are never good. The key is to be vigilant and purposeful in our walk with Christ, because the enemy uses many things to cleverly disguise and conceal this disease. When we allow complacency to take up residence in our lives the enemy has a foothold. It gives him places to quietly creep in as he sets his traps of destruction in an attempt to kill, steal, and destroy.

"Be sober, be vigilant, because your adversary the devil, as a roaring lion, walketh about seeking whom he may devour." (1 Peter 5:8, NIV)

So how do we avoid this dangerous pitfall? Be sober and vigilant. We cannot afford to leave any room for complacency. We must also remember what Beth said, "as Christians we need to agitate ourselves." To agitate means, "To put into violent motion; to shake briskly; to excite, consider, discuss." Wow, what a perfect description!

I believe Revelation 3:2, 3 holds important keys on how to avoid this ugly trap and maintain our zeal for the Lord. It says, "wake up, strengthen what remains, remember what we have received and heard," and lastly, "repent and obey!"

In closing, I want to leave you with Strong's Greek definitions of four important words: *sober, vigilant, strengthen,* and *remember.* Take some time to meditate on these words, then apply them to your life. Once you do, complacency will no longer have an opportunity to hinder your love walk between God and man.

Sober: To be sober, to be calm and collected in spirit; to be temperate, (calm, cool) dispassionate, circumspect, (watchful on all sides; wary, thoughtful).

Vigilant: To watch; give strict attention to, be cautious, active; to take heed lest through remission (relinquishment; give up) and indolence (laziness; idleness) some destructive calamity suddenly overtake one.

Strengthen: To make stable, place firmly, set fast, fix; to strengthen, make firm; to render constant, confirm one's mind.

Remember: To be mindful of, to remember, to call to mind; to think of and feel for a person or thing; to hold in memory, keep in mind; to make mention of.

Chapter 3

God Is in Control

"Even to your old age and gray hairs I am He, I am He who will sustain you. I have made you and I will carry you; I will sustain you and I will rescue you." (Isaiah 46:4, NIV)

Scripture Focus

"This is what the Lords says, your Redeemer, the Holy One of Israel: I am the Lord your God, who teaches you what is best for you, who directs you in the way you should go. If only you had paid attention to my commands, your peace would have been like a river, your righteousness like the waves of the sea." (Isaiah 48:17-18, NIV)

"Many are the woes of the wicked, but the Lord's unfailing love surrounds the man who trusts in Him. Rejoice in the Lord and be glad, you righteous; sing, all you who are upright in heart!" (Psalm 32:10-11, NIV)

"The eyes of the Lord are on the righteous, and His ears are attentive to their cry."
(Psalm 34:15, NIV)

"Be still and know that I am God..." (Psalm 46:10, NIV)

Bob's Story

By Bob Wilcox

While we were building our home in Florida, it came time to do the roof. I had some experience in roofing, but even for a professional roofer, this would have been a bit of a challenge. I felt somewhat anxious about doing it myself, not to mention it was July and *hot*!

On my way out to the property that morning, I purposed in my heart not to allow anything to rob me of another day of work. Up to that point, there had been numerous delays and difficulties to overcome, and although it wasn't raining yet, I could hear the thunder and see the lightning all around me. From the time we began building the house until now it had not rained, but on this day it appeared to be inevitable and the beginning of yet another aggravating delay.

It made no sense to be on the roof of a two-story building in Florida (the nation's lightning capital) during these conditions, but I refused to flinch! As I arrived, I gathered my tools and headed up to the roof to work. The more trips I made up and down the ladder more intense became the anger I felt toward the devil and his attempts to hinder my work. I began rebuking, binding, releasing…Just throwing a plain ole Holy Ghost fit; to the point I almost felt a little sorry for the devil, ha! Regardless, I would not succumb to any more delays.

As I began working I felt quite proud of the tongue-lashing I had given the devil, but after about thirty minutes or so, I gradually calmed down and came to my senses. It was then I heard that "still small voice" say something unexpected, as every word filled me with an indescribable humility and love: "I just thought you could use a breeze today."

At that moment I felt incredibly small, humbled, and convicted. How could I ascribe evil to the blessing God was trying to bring me? I immediately asked for forgiveness for looking at the circumstances and assuming this must be the hand of the enemy. That entire day it looked stormy with lightning and thunder all around, but it never rained a drop. In fact, a nice cool breeze surrounded me and God blessed me with a wonderful day.

The next morning I went back to work on the roof. Once again it proved to be a typical hot and humid mid-July day in Florida. By the time I carried all my tools up to the roof and prepared to go to work I was drenched in sweat, but this time I prayed a little differently: "Lord, you know that breeze yesterday? I sure could use it again today." In just a matter of minutes, clouds began forming, and the wind started blowing to the point I had to hold my ball cap on with one hand and proceed to roof with the other. Again, God blessed me with another wonderful day.

~The End~

Truth

This story is very dear to our hearts as we reflect on how the Lord revealed Himself to Bob. Throughout the entire process of building our first home together, God's hand remained faithful as He guided and protected Bob every step of the way. We shared many happy memories there before packing up and leaving for missionary school.

As I prepared for this chapter, I asked Bob what spoke to him the most during those moments. He said, "God knows what we have need of, but sometimes we get too caught up in appearances and circumstances. Then we begin assuming that everything we *perceive as negative* is of the devil, and *we fail to realize God is at work*. We need to trust Him and rest in His ability to work all things out for the good. We must learn not to assume, and to weigh our words before anything comes out of our mouths."

This is a powerful statement and full of wisdom. Just think what we might learn if we took our assumptions and perceptions to the Father before putting our mouths in motion! This experience and Bob's statement has certainly taught me a valuable lesson, and I am truly grateful.

We knew God methodically and beautifully orchestrated every aspect of our lives in the preparation of building our home, but there had been so many obstacles and distractions. Because we fixed our eyes on the circumstances there were times we forgot something very important; *God is in control!* When our schedule gets interrupted or the unexpected happens, like Bob, we often find ourselves stressed out and caught up in rebuking the enemy for what *we perceive* he is doing to us.

Take a moment and make a decision to take your assumptions and perceptions to God; then be quiet and listen! God knows what you need and He may be trying to get it to you right now, but He is hindered by the words coming out of your mouth! Allow the Holy Spirit to quiet your mind in an effort to bring a cool breeze or fresh cup of water you so desperately need.

Will you trust Him today to meet your needs and rest in His power to do the impossible? If you choose well, you will be blessed. Fix your eyes on Jesus, not on the circumstances or situation. Once you do this, get ready; a blessing is headed your way and you may be surprised how the Father delivers it! Remember what His Word says, "For My thoughts are not your thoughts, neither are your ways My ways, declares the Lord." (Isaiah 55:8, NIV)

Chapter 4

A Miracle in Ethiopia

"Therefore, since we are surrounded by such a great cloud of witnesses, let us throw off everything that hinders and the sins that so easily entangle, and let us run with perseverance the race marked out for us. Let us fix our eyes on Jesus, the Author and Perfecter of our faith, who for the joy set before Him endured the cross, scorning its shame, and sat down at the right hand of the Throne of God. Consider Him who endured such opposition from sinful men, so that you will not grow weary and lose heart." (Hebrews 12:1-3, NIV)

Scripture Focus

"For God so loved the world that He gave His one and only Son, that whoever believes in Him shall not perish but have eternal life. For God did not send His Son into the world to condemn the world, but to save the world through Him. Whoever believes in Him is not condemned, but whoever does not believe stands condemned already because he has not believed in the name of God's one and only Son.

"This is the verdict: Light has come into the world, but men loved darkness instead of light because their deeds were evil. Everyone who does evil hates the light, and will not come into the light for fear that his deeds will be exposed. But whoever lives by the truth comes into the light, so that it may be seen plainly that what he has done has been done through God." (John 3:16-21, NIV)

Grandmother's Encounter with God

By Abel Taye and Frehiwot Taye

My name is Abel Taye, and I am from Ethiopia. I came to this country to complete missionary school as well as my formal education. Missionary school is where I first met Bob and Donna, and the Lord created a special bond between us from the very beginning. In fact, I consider them my American Mom and Dad.

In May of 2006, I received a Bachelor of Science degree from Colorado Christian University in organizational management with an emphasis on human resources, and I am planning to continue my studies to obtain a master's and PhD. My desire is to return to my country and work in the political arena in an effort to spread the message of Jesus Christ to my people. My vision is to see my country turn to God through the youth of Ethiopia. Bob and Donna are supportive of my vision and have never stopped believing in me. It has been amazing to see the hand of God at work in the relationships He has blessed me with over the past few years.

My mother (Frehiwot Taye) came from Ethiopia for my graduation ceremony at Colorado Christian University, and she met my American parents for the first time. I only wish my father and siblings could have come over as well. I pray one day that will be possible, but for now, I am looking forward to returning to Ethiopia in the near future and taking Bob and Donna home with me for an extended visit. What an amazing time we will have when that day arrives!

It was during Mother's visit that Mama Donna asked me to write the story of my Grandmother and her final days before going to meet the Lord. Mother assisted me with the details, since she was with her during her final moments on this earth. Due to a lack of finances and ministry obligations, I could not return to Ethiopia during her illness and passing; however, God brought comfort and peace to my spirit in a wonderful way. He is a faithful Father. I pray this miraculous story of Grandmother's final days encourages your heart, for it truly testifies of God's awesome power!

Grandmother's name is Dejytenu Zechargrachew, and she was born in a small village in a town called Ambo, Ethiopia. She grew up in a very religious Orthodox background (one that closes the door to the Gospel). Grandmother was a very generous woman with an out-going personality, which made her popular and loved by many people in her hometown.

My mother was the one who brought Jesus to our entire family in Ethiopia, and five years prior to Grandmother's death, she, too, accepted the Lord. Due to her very conservative background, she followed Jesus in a secret way, much like Nicodemus in the Gospel of John.

Grandmother became seriously ill of cancer, and the doctor advised Mom to prepare for the worst. Everyone in our family is very close, and they had a difficult time accepting the situation. Some of them brought what they called *holy water* from the surrounding Orthodox communities and attempted other religious practices, hoping for a miracle.

During all of this Mom prayed for the Lord to give her confirmation about Grandmother's salvation. As the days progressed, the situation deteriorated, and Grandmother stopped eating and drinking. She could no longer move or communicate, and even breathing proved difficult and painful for her. With each passing hour, things grew more critical.

One morning Mom went to her bedside and laid her hands on Grandmother. She asked her to say just one thing: "Jesus is Lord."

My Grandmother responded with signs and in a very low, frail voice (speaking in Amharic, the Ethiopian national language) said, "Jesus is Lord." As she kept trying to utter those words, she appeared suddenly energized and began repeatedly stating, "Countless are your angels, Lord!" Then she started repeating, "How beautiful is your sword, Jesus!"

As this encounter with God continued, Grandmother's voice grew louder and stronger, and she began speaking in a foreign language that no one understood. Then, she spoke in English and said, "Jesus, check my name!" Everyone knew this was a miracle because she had never spoken in English before. Mother believes during this miraculous encounter with God that Grandmother saw the *Book of Life*.

As these things continued to happen, the two relatives who were in the room next to Grandmother's bed were shocked. They knew that she had not been able to move, talk, open her eyes, and especially speak in English or a foreign language! In amazement they stated, "This is a spirit, not from human action!"

Within two weeks, my seventy-four-year-old grandmother went to be with the Lord, and Mom was so grateful for the way God miraculously answered her prayers. Our family knows that we will all be together again one day in heaven. Having that assurance we say, "Hallelujah and Amen!"

~The End~

Truth

We are so proud of our Ethiopian son, Abel. His faith and commitment to God has been a blessing and inspiration. For the devotion portion of this chapter, I want to focus on something Abel referred to in reference to his Grandmother; the story of Jesus and Nicodemus. It beautifully explains the process of being *born again* and the incredible sacrifice God made by sending His One and only Son to die on a cruel cross for our sins.

I am so thankful the cross was not the end. His death and resurrection was the beginning for all of us to experience salvation and so much more while we are on this earthly journey. And when this part of our journey has ended, accepting Jesus Christ as our Lord and Savior gives us the assurance of spending eternity with Him in Heaven. This hope brings a glorious peace to my heart and soul!

Jesus Teaches Nicodemus

"Now there was a man of the Pharisees named Nicodemus, a member of the Jewish ruling council. He came to Jesus at night and said, "Rabbi, we know you are a teacher who has come from God. For no one could perform the miraculous signs you are doing if God were not with him." In reply Jesus declared, "I tell you the truth, no one can see the kingdom of God unless he is born again."

"How can a man be born when he is old?" Nicodemus asked. "Surely he cannot enter a second time into his mother's womb to be born!" Jesus

answered, "I tell you the truth, no one can enter the kingdom of God unless he is born of water and the Spirit. Flesh gives birth to flesh, but the Spirit gives birth to spirit. You should not be surprised at my saying, 'You must be born again.' The wind blows wherever it pleases. You hear its sound, but you cannot tell where it comes from or where it is going. So it is with everyone born of the Spirit."
(John 3:1-8, NIV)

Jesus tells us in our first birth we are "born of water." Typically, before giving birth the pregnant woman's sac of protective, amniotic fluid (her water) is broken; which gives us an understanding to the phrase, "born of water." Jesus uses similar terminology in John 3:6, affirming His prior statement when he says, "Flesh gives birth to flesh, but the Spirit gives birth to spirit." We all experience the first birth, "born of water," for we are all flesh.

In our second birth, we are "born of the Spirit." Our first birth leads to death, but our second birth leads to eternal life. Our earthly bodies will someday die; however, our spirit will live on in Heaven if we have accepted Jesus Christ as our Lord and Savior. In Romans 6:4 it says the new birth is a new beginning that results in "newness of life."

Verse 21 of John chapter 3 states, "But whoever lives by the truth comes into the light, so that it may be seen plainly that what he has done has been done through God." Before Abel's Grandmother went to be with Jesus, she was able to give a powerful testimony in an unforgettable way. God truly received the glory because of the miracle that happened in that room for the entire family to witness.

The Lord answered Abel's mother's prayer, and He will do the same for you. If you are praying for someone to receive the gift of salvation, healing, or restoration, then you must persevere and continue interceding. Refuse to give up! Intercession is a precious gift all of us can experience and should actively participate in. God does not ignore the persistent, intercessory prayers of His people. We should all desire to reach the lost with the knowledge of Christ and His power to save, heal, and restore!

Let's look again at John 3:16-21, and this time I will use the New Living Translation. As you read the passage, take time to meditate on what the scriptures are saying and give praise for this amazing gift God gave us through His one and only Son, Jesus Christ.

"For God loved the world so much that He gave His one and only Son, so that *everyone who believes in Him will not perish but have eternal life. God sent His Son into the world not to judge the world, but to save the world through Him.* There is no judgment against anyone who believes in Him. But anyone who does not believe in Him has already been judged for not believing in God's one and only Son. And the judgment is based on this fact: God's light came into the world, but people loved the darkness more than the light, for their actions were evil. *All who do evil hate the light and refuse to go near it for fear their sins will be exposed. But those who do what is right come to the light so others can see that they are doing what God wants."* (John 3:16-21, NLT, Emphasis added)

If you have not accepted Jesus Christ as your Savior, there is no time like the present; however, it is important to have an understanding of what you are doing. This prayer is effective and life changing when people know, understand, and believe they are sinners in need of salvation. The Bible tells us we are all sinners: "As it is written, 'There is none righteous, no, not one." (Romans 3:10, KJV). Because of our sins, we deserve eternal punishment (Matthew 25:46). The sinner's prayer is a simple but powerful request for grace and mercy instead of wrath and judgment (Titus 3:5-7).

Regardless of what some beliefs teach, good works cannot save us! The standard by which truth is based is solely upon God's Word. The Bible tells us, "For it is by grace you have been saved, through faith— and this not from yourselves, it is the gift of God—**not by works, so that no one can boast."** (Ephesians 2:8-9, NIV, emphasis added).

Be careful what you choose to believe! Oprah may think all paths lead to God, but the Bible clearly states there is *only one way to Heaven and that is through Christ!* "Jesus answered, 'I am the Way the Truth, and the Life. *No one comes to the Father except through Me."* (John 14:6, NIV, emphasis added).

Romans 10:9 simplifies this process by saying; "That if you confess with your mouth, 'Jesus is Lord,' and believe in your heart that God raised Him from the dead, you will be saved."

The Father is waiting with arms open wide and they are full of love, forgiveness, and blessings beyond comprehension. Take a moment and consider praying the following prayer of salvation. If you choose to take this step of faith, get ready for a miracle because your life will never be the same!

Prayer

"Lord Jesus, I believe You are the Son of God. Thank You for dying on the cross for my sins. I acknowledge that I am a sinner in need of salvation. Please forgive my sins, and give me the gift of eternal life. I am asking You to come into my heart, and I give You permission to be the Lord and Savior of my life. I want to serve You and walk in Your ways. Please give me wisdom and understanding as I read and study Your Word. Teach me how to apply it to my life. Thank You for this precious gift. I love You!"

Welcome to the Family of God! The Bible tells us the angels in Heaven rejoice when one receives Jesus Christ as their Lord and Savior. You are now a brand new creation: "Therefore, if anyone is in Christ, he is a new creation; the old has gone, the new has come!" (Corinthians 5:17, NIV).

You are God's child, and He is your Father. What does this mean? It means every promise and blessing that is in the Bible belongs to you! "Yet to all who received Him, to those who believed in His name, He gave the right to become children of God." (John 1:12, NIV)

We must understand an important fact; we live in a fallen world. Becoming a Christian does not mean everything is suddenly perfect and nothing bad will ever happen. Life will continue to dish out pain and sorrow, but do not fret! God is your Father and He is in control. His Word will guide you to a path of joy unspeakable, wisdom and knowledge beyond your own human intellect, and peace in the midst of the storm.

But wait, there is more! The Lord also gloriously delivers His children, brings victory in the face of defeat, and lovingly supplies the keys to living an overcoming life through His Word and His mighty hand of power and justice. *What more could you possibly want?*

You are probably wondering; *What should I do now that I have prayed the sinner's prayer and accepted Christ as my Savior?* Good question! By following these next four steps you will begin experiencing an amazing new life. Stay the course; you are a child of a powerful and faithful Father. He can do anything *but* fail. *Nothing is impossible with the Great I Am, your Creator!*

1. **Read your Bible every day. Only then will you be able to get to know Christ, understand His character, and form a relationship with Him.**

"Your Word is a lamp to my feet and a light for my path." (Psalm 119:105, NIV)

"Do your best to present yourself to God as one approved, a workman who does not need to be ashamed and who correctly handles the Word of Truth." (2 Timothy 2:15, NIV)

2. **Talk to God in prayer every day just like you would talk to your best friend.**

"Do not be anxious about anything, but in everything, by prayer and petition, with thanksgiving present your requests to God." (Philippians 4:6, NIV)

3. **Be baptized, worship, fellowship, and serve the Lord with other Christians.** Become part of a church where Christ is preached, and the Bible is the final and only authority!

"Let us not give up meeting together, as some are in the habit of doing, but let us encourage one another—and all the more as you see the Day approaching." (Hebrews 10:25, NIV)

"Whoever believes and is baptized will be saved, but whoever does not believe will be condemned." (Mark 16:16, NIV)

"Peter replied, "Repent and be baptized, every one of you, in the name of Jesus Christ for the forgiveness of your sins. And you will receive the gift of the Holy Spirit. The promise is for you and your children and for all who are far off—for all whom the Lord our God will call…. Those who accepted his message were baptized, and about three thousand were added to their number that day." (Acts 2:38-39, 41, NIV)

4. Tell others about Christ!

"I am not ashamed of the gospel, because it is the power of God for the salvation of everyone who believes." (Romans 1:16, NIV)

"He said to them, "Go into all the world and preach the good news to all creation." (Mark 16:15, NIV)

"Therefore go and make disciples of all nations, baptizing them in the name of the Father and the Son and of the Holy Spirit." (Matthew 28:19, NIV)

Abel and Bob, Graduation Day

Abel and Donna, Graduation Day

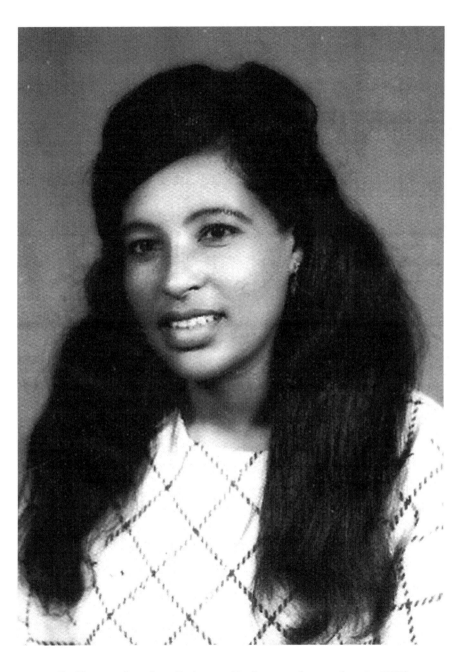

Abel's grandmother, Dejytenu Zechargrachew, taken in 1970

Chapter 5

Prayer and Worry, a Bad Combination!

"For He will command His angels concerning you to guard you in all your ways." (Psalm 91:11, NIV)

Scripture Focus

"The name of the Lord is a strong tower; the righteous runneth into it, and is safe." (Proverbs 18:10, KJV)

"...Fear not, for I have redeemed you; I have summoned you by name; you are Mine. When you pass through the waters, I will be with you; and when you pass through the rivers, they will not sweep over you. When you walk through the fire, you will not be burned; the flames will not set you ablaze. For I am the Lord, your God, the Holy One of Israel, your Savior." (Isaiah 43:1-3, NIV)

"He shall not be afraid of evil tidings; his heart is fixed, trusting in the Lord." (Psalm 112:7, KJV)

"I will lie down and sleep in peace, for You alone, O Lord, make me dwell in safety." (Psalm 4:8, NIV)

"The Lord is my light and my salvation; whom shall I fear? The Lord is the strength of my life; of whom shall I be afraid?" (Psalm 27:1, NIV)

"But let all that take refuge in You be glad; let them ever sing for joy. Spread Your protection over them that those who love Your name may rejoice in You. For surely, O Lord, You bless the righteous; You surround them with Your favor as with a shield." (Psalm 5:11, 12, NIV)

Traci's Story

By Traci Wilcox

My name is Traci Wilcox. I am Bob's daughter, and Donna is my stepmom. My story is about something that happened during my first year as a student at Auburn University.

I was on the Flag Corps team, and for one of our games we traveled to Atlanta for the Auburn vs. Georgia Tech game. After the game was over the Tech fans rushed the field and started tearing down the goal posts. As we were trying to leave the stands, my friend Elizabeth and I saw this man (whom we did not know) wearing a Georgia Tech Jersey. He called our names, pulling us out of the aisle. Just as we moved, a piece of the goal post landed right where we had been standing, and everyone started rushing to the top of the stairs.

Everything happened so fast, but when we got to the top we tried to find this person to thank him, but he mysteriously disappeared. We quickly realized something else; we were not wearing anything on our clothing with our names on it. We were in a different City and State, and neither one of us knew anyone from Georgia Tech. We could not help but wonder, *How did he know our names and who was this man? Could he have been an angel?*

A few days later, I called my dad and said, "Dad, an angel saved my life." I shared with him what happened and felt blessed to know God was looking out for me.

~The End~

Truth

The year Bob and I left Florida to go into missions Traci graduated from high school. It proved to be a difficult time for Bob, because if something happened to his little girl he would be far, far away. Traci had an exciting future ahead of her as she made plans to attend Auburn University. She was a young woman embarking on her own new adventure, but in a daddy's mind age does not matter. You see, a dad always pictures his daughter as *his little girl.* The fact is, my dad still sees me as his baby and I am a middle-aged woman!

So what is a parent to do? For the Believer we should line our life and actions up with God's Word; therefore, we must pray in faith for our children and refuse to succumb to doubt and fear. Giving into feelings of fear will only result in one thing, worry! Bob made a decision not to entertain thoughts of fear and worry, and I admired his unwavering faith and resolve in God's ability to take care of Traci. Watching Bob increased my faith in a huge way when I prayed for family, friends, and all the young people God allowed us to parent and love. Together, we faithfully claimed Psalm 91:11 over our loved ones, asking God to send His angels to protect and watch over them. The night Traci called and told her dad what happened, we both shed joyous tears over how beautifully God answered our prayers!

In May of 2007, Traci graduated from Auburn University with honors. Bob could hardly hold back tears as he watched his little girl (who suddenly looked all grown up), graduate from College with a nursing degree. We were both so proud of the accomplishments and choices Traci made for her life in order to fulfill her dream of becoming a nurse. Although distance still separates us, prayer has no boundaries and we know God will continue to protect and direct her steps.

When you have worrisome thoughts and behaviors, you must realize this is a brain and mind issue. Christ gives us some important keys to overcoming worry in Philippians, chapter 4; "Don't worry about anything; instead, pray about everything. Tell God what you need, and thank him for all He has done. Then you will experience God's peace, which exceeds anything we can understand. His peace will guard your hearts and minds as you live in Christ Jesus. And now, dear brothers and sisters, one final thing. Fix your thoughts on what is true, and honorable, and right, and pure, and lovely, and admirable. Think about things that are excellent and worthy of praise. Keep putting into practice all you learned and received from me—everything you heard from me and saw me doing. *Then the God of peace will be with you.*" (Philippians 4:6-9, NLT, emphasis added).

The Bible also directs us to put into practice *the fruit of the Spirit*; "But the fruit of the Spirit is love, joy, peace, forbearance, kindness, goodness, faithfulness, gentleness and self-control. Against such things there is no law." (Galatians 5:22, 23, NIV). Christ never commands us to do something that is impossible to accomplish. We **can** choose to practice self-control and take captive every thought. We have been given the gift of choice, and it is up to us to choose well!

Many things in this life can create difficult mental challenges when it comes to fighting against doubt, fear, and worry; however, we must remember how powerful our Father is and His amazing ability to hear and answer prayer. As Believers, we should pray a *prayer covering* over our loved ones, and then leave them in the Father's faithful and loving hands. It truly is a faith thing and God responds to faith!

"And without faith it is impossible to please God, because anyone who comes to Him must believe that He exists and that He rewards those who earnestly seek Him." (Hebrews 11:6, NIV)

"But the righteous will live by his faith." (Habakkuk 2:4, NIV)

"And everything that does not come from faith is sin." (Romans 14:23, NIV)

"So that your faith might not rest on men's wisdom, but on God's power." (1 Corinthians 2:5, NIV)

Does having faith in God mean bad things will not happen? No. But we can rest in the knowledge that our Heavenly Father is always in control. He will give us the grace and wisdom to walk through whatever circumstances life presents. He alone can take those things meant to destroy and devastate, and bring forth something of beauty, blessing, and wisdom. By consistently turning our concerns and problems over to God, we will experience and understand the importance of overcoming those three unproductive words: *fear, doubt,* and *worry.*

Prior to leaving Florida, I spoke at a women's conference about *prayer coverings* and all the scriptures of protection God has given us. As I studied for the conference I became so convicted of the times I prayed for God to send His angels to guard and protect those I love, only to turn around and start worrying all over again. The Bible is full of faith-filled scriptures and promises on this subject, and yet I somehow allowed myself to be consumed with worry. Why? Did I trust God or not? I am ashamed to admit it, but my words said, "Yes," yet my actions clearly said, "No!"

Realizing and admitting this truth helped me to seek repentance and begin speaking God's Word with authority in Jesus' name every time doubt, fear, and worry attempted to consume and invade my mind. It truly changed how I prayed and opened my eyes to the incredible power which engulfs our lives when we begin casting down imaginations and thoughts that do not line up with scripture. I became careful about what *I chose* to allow my mind to dwell and focus on. By putting this into practice, my faith greatly increased and an overwhelming peace replaced fear, doubt, and worry.

This continues to be something I must regularly *choose* to do. The only way to cultivate success is to daily study the scriptures and fill my heart and mind with the Word of God. It is vital for us to saturate ourselves with God's truth so that the banner of faith is raised high when fear and doubt try to creep in and overtake our minds with worry.

Unfortunately, we are constantly bombarded with messages of fear from the media and so many other sources. If all we ever do is watch news reports about all the horrible things that are happening in the world and surf the Internet for the latest bad news, then fear and worry will overpower us. It is a battle, and the only weapon against it is the living, breathing Word of God; along with our decision to believe and trust the Lord to be a true and faithful Father. Let me offer some advice: turn off the television and computer, put down the newspaper, open up the Bible and begin reading. The next step is to apply God's truth to your life. Application is the key.

Let me give you an example of application. If you have a wound that needs antibiotic ointment to prevent infection and a Band-Aid to protect it; then you must apply the ointment and take the Band-Aid out of the box, open it and cover the wound. You can read the directions and educate yourself on the benefits of these products, but if you place the items in your medicine cabinet and never apply them, it won't do you any good at all! Think about it for a moment; the results you are seeking are in the application. Reading God's Word but never applying it to your life will leave you frustrated, empty, and unprotected; therefore, doubt, fear, and worry are inevitable.

"So also faith, if it does not have works [deeds and actions of obedience to back it up], by itself is destitute of power [inoperative, dead]." (James 2:17, AMP)

Let's talk about worry? Is it beneficial? The answer is, no! It will not change your situation except to add additional problems and anxiety. It can also cause ulcers, panic attacks, along with other physical, emotional, and mental health issues. Studies conducted over a period of twenty years have proven the negative effects of *worry* on a person's mind and body. The results have rendered an exhaustive list of pain and suffering. As a Chaplain and Counselor, I continuously provide education along with healthy options and strategies regarding the issues of fear and worry, yet many continue to make a choice to give into it.

The Word of God is very clear on the subject of worry. The Bible is so direct that even a child can hear and understand. It is up to us to apply what we read and make healthy choices. No one can do it for us.

"Therefore, I tell you, do not worry about your life, what you will eat or drink, or about your body, what you will wear. Is not life more important than food, and the body more important than clothes? Look at the birds of the air; they do not sow or reap or store away in barns, and yet your Heavenly Father feeds them. Are you not much more valuable than they? *Who of you by worrying can add a single hour to his life?*

And why do you worry about clothes? See how the lilies of the field grow. They do not labor or spin. Yet I tell you that not even Solomon in all his splendor was dressed like one of these. If that is how God clothes the grass of the field, which is here today and tomorrow is thrown into the fire, will He not much more clothe you, *O you of little faith?* So do not worry, saying, 'What shall we eat?' or 'What shall we drink?' or 'What shall we wear?' For the pagans run after all these things, and *your Heavenly Father knows that you need them.* But seek first His kingdom and His righteousness, and all these things will be given to you as well. *Therefore, do not worry about tomorrow, for tomorrow will worry about itself.* Each day has enough trouble of its own." (Matthew 6:25-34, NIV, emphasis added)

Let us take a moment to evaluate what we have learned. First, the choice is ours! To avoid worry we must give our concerns and issues to God, and refuse to pick them back up. Second, practice applying what the scriptures teach. Application begins when we commit *everything* and *everyone* to daily prayer and intercession. And finally, trust God with the outcome!

The most important ingredient in prayer is *faith*. With faith comes the desire to make application. It is not difficult to apply what we read, *but it is a choice!* Regardless of the circumstances, hold on tightly to the truth of God's Word. Then, take a step of faith by speaking scriptures of protection, peace, healing (whatever the case may be), over your situation. Doubts will come and worry will try to creep in, but do not allow yourself to entertain worst-case scenarios. With unwavering faith, believe God hears and answers your prayers. He is still a miracle working, powerful Father who loves His children!

"For everyone who asks, receives. Everyone who seeks, finds. And to everyone who knocks, the door will be opened. You parents—if your children ask for a loaf of bread, do you give them a stone instead? Or if they ask for a fish, do you give them a snake? Of course not! So if you sinful people know how to give good gifts to your children, how much more will your heavenly Father give good gifts to those who ask him." (Matthew 7:8-11, NLT)

To change a habit and **retrain** the way we think takes time, determination, and faithful diligence; *but you can do it!* We are not alone because Christ our Lord is with and for us. His Word promises, "For I can do everything through Christ, who gives me strength." (Philippians 4:13, NLT). In and through Christ we have the power and wisdom to overcome those three ugly and unproductive words: doubt, fear, and worry!

Traci's graduation from Auburn University in 2007

Chapter 6

Overcoming Depression

"The LORD is a refuge for the oppressed, a stronghold in times of trouble. Those who know Your name will trust in You, for You, LORD, have never forsaken those who seek You." (Psalm 9: 9-10, NIV)

Scripture Focus

"It is the Lord who goes before you; He will [march] with you; He will not fail you or let you go or forsake you; [let there be no cowardice or flinching, but] fear not, neither become broken [in spirit—depressed, dismayed, and unnerved with alarm]. (Deuteronomy 31:8, AMP)

"ARISE [from the depression and prostration in which circumstances have kept you—rise to a new life]! Shine (be radiant with the glory of the Lord), for your light has come, and the glory of the Lord has risen upon you." (Isaiah 60:1, AMP)

"But God, who comforts and encourages and refreshes and cheers the depressed and the sinking, comforted and encouraged and refreshed and cheered us." (2 Corinthians 7:6, AMP)

"Casting the whole of your care [all your anxieties, all your worries, all your concerns, once and for all] on Him, for He cares for you affectionately and cares about you watchfully." (1 Peter 5:6-7, AMP)

Freedom!

By Laura Marie Burt

I can remember having it since the age of seven. It became a part of my fragile identity as minutes turned into moments, moments to hours, and hours to what seemed like an eternity of despair. Depression had become my constant companion, and life without it seemed impossible, or so I thought.

I am from the South Bay area of California, a city called Torrance. I grew up in a Christian home, but during my childhood my family did not know the freedom and confidence that can be experienced in Christ. My mom had been diagnosed with bipolar disorder at a young age, and later my older sister was diagnosed with it as well. Mom seemed affected mostly with the depression side of bipolar and often found herself struggling just to get through the day. My dad stayed busy with work, and when he did have time for us I dreaded it. He was very controlling and lectured us kids constantly for what seemed to be the most insignificant things. Life at my house felt far from perfect.

Not long after I turned seven something wonderful happened; my little sister was born. The thought of having a little sister both delighted and excited me. It may sound cheesy, but I remember carrying around a little pin my mother gave me with my little sister's picture on it, in proud declaration that I had become a big sister.

The excitement and newness of this little demanding creature faded fast as I realized I was disappearing into the background of my family's attention. I often remained in my room hoping that someone would come find me, but no one showed up. It seemed no one cared, and I felt forgotten. Time went on, and nothing changed. I continued to slip deeper into despair and depression, along with a bitter and lonely cycle of negative thoughts.

Dysfunction became more and more familiar to my family. In fact, that is what I thought a "normal" home was like. The pain grew, and so did my downward spiral of depression. I spent many nights alone in my room, which became the breeding ground for Satan's lies to multiply and take root in my heart and mind. In this isolated state, I began to believe no one loved me and that God must not either. I soon realized something else; I pretty much wasn't my biggest fan either. In fact, I despised myself. My thoughts went something like this: *If only I was prettier maybe people would notice me*, or, *If I was sweeter or funnier I'd be more lovable and less easy to forget. If only...*

Life went on, and although my circumstances told me that God had abandoned and forgotten me, He never stopped pursuing me! Even through junior high, when I tried to pretend He didn't exist, He continued to be a loving and jealous God after my heart. Finally, in ninth grade I met a girl who became a friend, and she invited me to church. Her family took me in and lovingly showed me the love of Christ in a manifest form. I got plugged into a church, and God began speaking to my heart. I actually started listening to what He was saying and had been speaking to me along. As God continuously showed me His love, I struggled with being able to receive the love of Christ, but that did not stop the Lord's pursuit! He faithfully and patiently endured my stubborn resistance, even when I felt unlovable and repeatedly pushed Him away.

During this time, depression had turned into a consistent and debilitating presence. Even the minutest tasks in life such as brushing my teeth or getting out of bed felt overwhelming and painful. I slept all the time, and yet I remained in a constant state of being tired—just plain weary. I felt invisible, as though I barely existed; however, I watched other people living their lives. My life had no purpose. I basically knew that in order to move I must put one foot in front of the next. I lived in a state of survival and numbness. I often awoke in the mornings depressed and mad. Life had become a daily battle that I usually lost.

As days turned into months and months to years, I slowly but surely grew in the love of God. By the age of seventeen the Lord had really brought me a long way. He continued to bring healing to my wounds and teach me about His will and purpose for my life, yet I still struggled with depression. By this time, I didn't question its presence in my life because it had become such a familiar companion for so many years.

I soon graduated from high school and decided to join YWAM (Youth with a Mission) and do a school called DTS (Discipleship Training School) in Weston, Colorado. This is where I met Bob and Donna Wilcox. They embraced me with an unconditional love and treated me as if I were their very own child. Their mentoring and support left a lasting and positive effect on my physical and emotional life, but more importantly on my spiritual life. God gave us a very special bond, and they continue to be like parents to me to this very day!

One day as Mama Donna and I were taking a walk, I had been in a bit of a low slump, and I began telling her about it. At one point in the conversation she said something that I will never forget. It was a simple but true statement that revolutionized the way I lived my life from that point on. She said to me, "Laura, you know you don't have to live with depression; it is not who you are!" She said much more as we walked together that day, but that one line stuck in my mind and stayed with me, even today!

I had lived with depression for so long, and the belief that I did not have to continue to receive this unwanted companion never truly crossed my mind, especially while living in a family that seemed to embrace mental illness and depression as normalcy; to not accept it was a foreign concept to me.

After my DTS and spending two months in Kenya on a mission's outreach, I headed back home to California to live with my family. I needed to figure out what to do with my life. This turned out to be one of the hardest seasons I ever experienced, because the depression intensified greatly. Yet God had given me the hope of healing and freedom from this horrible affliction, and I wasn't about to give up now.

The path towards God's healing was messy and far from perfect, but whenever I faltered and felt overwhelmed with despair, I turned my eyes back to Christ. I began to worship and praise the Lord *in advance* for the healing and freedom He was going to bring me.

One particularly bad day, I remember feeling utterly crippled by depression. I sat on the edge of my bed wondering if I'd ever be healed. I thought to myself. *Maybe this is just a part of me, and I'll never be any different. What if I am fighting in vain?* Soon after that, I remember talking to a good friend, and she told me, *Laura, even if God never heals you from depression, and you have this crippling disorder for the rest of your life, will you still serve and love Him?* As I stood there facing this huge unanswered question, I made a decision that I have never regretted. I purposed in my heart to serve God even if He never healed me, and I also decided I wasn't going to give up believing that He could heal me! I knew deep down in my heart that the sacrifice Christ made on the cross so that we can be redeemed, healed, and so much more, meant that He wanted to heal me even more than I wanted it!

After I spent nine months in California, God suddenly gave me confirmation about my future and a new direction for life. I felt led to enroll at Bethany College of Missions in Minnesota. After much prayer and Christian council I felt it was the right thing to do, so *in faith* I quit my job, packed up my room, said good-bye to friends and family, and headed off to Minnesota.

My time at Bethany was a gift from the Lord. As I sought hard after God, it not only became a time for me to gain some independence, but most important, to receive healing and love from Jesus my Savior, Healer, and Redeemer! However, this would be a long journey filled with many challenges, because I soon discovered this battle of depression still raged within me. It didn't stay in California; like a shadow, it followed me to Bethany as I continued to experience days of falling on my face and being caught in a cycle of depression, despair, and negativity.

As I grew stronger in God's love those days of falling my face became fewer and fewer. One day I went to a prayer chapel at Bethany College, and a lady got up at one point and gave a prophetic word of knowledge. She stated she felt someone in the room had a negative pattern of thinking, and God wanted to break that downward cycle of thoughts and replace them with His thoughts. I immediately knew she was talking about me. I began praising God for His healing and thanking Him for not abandoning me.

During this time at school, I sought out a mentor and confided in her concerning my struggle with depression. Her name just happened to be Laura as well. Laura offered encouragement and said she would be there for me to hold up my hands to God, even when I felt too weak to do it myself. She told me she believed in the power of Jesus Christ that dwelt within me. She made a promise to stick by me through my time at Bethany and my struggles with depression. When things got rough, I called her or went to her house, and she always spoke God's truth to me. This proved to be powerful and necessary, because my mind continued to be bombarded with Satan's lies.

This went on for about a year at Bethany. I still experienced mornings where I woke up depressed and hating myself. I often had thoughts like, *Today is going to be horrible.* And guess what. It would be! One morning I woke up feeling this way. I felt horrible and upset. As I quickly got dressed and started walking over to the building where my classes were, I thought to myself, *Man, this day is going to be horrible. I hate today!* Immediately I realized something. Today really *was* going to be horrible if I didn't change my thinking. It just suddenly hit me: *This is ultimately my choice. Am I going to agree with the enemy that this day is horrible and pointless, or am I going to praise God and make a choice that this is going to be a good day?* I said to myself, *NO! Today is going to be a good day,* and I began praising God for this day that He had made. Guess what. It ended up being a good one!

The Lord completely healed me of depression sometime in my sophomore year at Bethany College. When people asked me how He healed me I simply tell them, *I just walked out of it!* I'm not even sure the exact moment it happened; all I know is I fixed my eyes on Christ and made a daily choice to agree with His Word.

Through consistently turning back to Jesus and trusting in His ability and power to do what seemed to be the impossible, I finally woke up and realized that by His precious blood I had been set free from depression, and I have continued to walk in freedom ever since!

First, I didn't give up. I chose to believe God not only had the power to heal me, but He wanted to heal me. Second, even in the hard times I praised God and spoke His truth *out loud.* Even when I did not feel like it, I continuously recited Bible verses pertaining to healing and began singing and praising God for the healing that I knew would come. Third, I learned the importance of *aligning myself with God's truth every day.* You see, I finally realized I had a choice in the matter, and I wanted to choose Christ and His truths for my life, rather than agreeing with the enemy!

~The End~

Truth

Like Laura, many of us have walked through the valley of depression and struggled with low self-esteem issues. In fact, the majority of young people God has brought into our lives have faced this battle. Because of Jesus Christ and His power and ability to heal, restore, and perform the miraculous, *we have overcome and we are overcomers!*

Laura is a precious young lady, and from the first moment we met it became evident God brought her into our family for a very special purpose. Bob and I are immensely grateful for every child and young person God has brought our way, and we appreciate their decision to stick around and become part of this huge family we enjoy so much. Together we have faced many difficult challenges and heart-wrenching moments; but the laughter, love, and growth have made it worth it all!

In September of 2007, we proudly watched our beautiful Laura graduate from Bethany College with a Bachelor of Arts degree in Cross-Cultural Studies. I wept tears of joy knowing how hard she fought to achieve this goal.

Over the years we witnessed God perform an amazing transformation as He brought healing to the hurts and wounds in Laura's life. The Father truly turned her ashes into beauty, and it did not happen by accident. Pay close attention to what she said at the end of her story. "I made a decision every day to align myself with God's truth. I finally realized I had a choice in the matter, and I wanted to choose Christ and His truths for my life, rather than agreeing with the enemy!"

Through perseverance, stubborn determination, and speaking God's truth, Laura received a miracle. She has such a heart for others and is a witness to young girls suffering from the same things she once battled. She has overcome many obstacles, but through it all, Laura is using her testimony in a powerful way to touch hearts and lives for Jesus Christ.

Our respect for Laura continued to grow as Bob and I witnessed her determination to break free from bondage. She desperately wanted deliverance. Her desire for healing created a hunger in Laura to embrace God's Word, as she began taking a serious look into every aspect of her life. This is a difficult process. You see, to experience genuine results a person must be willing to face the giants in their life with sincere honesty.

Then you must learn how to change your thinking and actually choose to do something about it!

To accomplish this task it is important to prepare for spiritual warfare. It is not a journey for the faint of heart. Breaking free from the generational curses handed down throughout your family, and grasping hold of the importance of renewing your mind in Christ on a daily (and sometimes minute-by-minute) basis is filled with challenges and pain. Once you take this step of faith your outlook will never be the same. As you begin seeing positive results, defeat and negative thinking will no longer dominate and control your existence.

As I prepared for this chapter I spent long, sleepless hours in prayer and research. First, I reflected upon the many years I have worked in the mental-health field and observed firsthand the miraculous results patients received when they cried out to God for help. God has given men and women wisdom to help those who are sick emotionally and physically, but we are mere humans. The greatest results are achieved when a partnership is formed between God and man. Second, I strategically investigated the positions and teachings of institutes and doctors who are not affiliated with Christianity, and several things caught my attention as I studied their findings. They share numerous common perceptions and key points concerning depression that Christian Counselors embrace.

As a mental health professional, I have seen many painful and debilitating effects caused from depression and other mental health disorders; however, our Heavenly Father is the Maker and Creator of our minds and bodies. He alone intricately created this amazing thing we call "our brain" and the remarkable machine we call "our body." Father God completed this task with more intelligence and attention to detail than any mere human being will ever comprehend!

Incredibly, all Believers have direct access to the very One who holds the answers to all of those perplexing issues we all face at some point in life, including deliverance from depression. A counselor who uses God's Word as their foundation when creating an action plan for their patient's total health and well-being, will experience success and break-through!

I want to pay close attention and analyze each one of the three common viewpoints on the subject of depression that are shared by experts in the mental health field. As we go through each one, it will astound you to discover how their findings line up with the Word of God. After we have gained a general understanding about depression and its causes, then we will look to the Bible for answers on how to break free from this curse and find healing.

Before we begin, make a decision to receive and apply this information to your life. *Remember, there is power is in application. You are not alone. Jesus Christ will guide you through to victory. In and through Him, You CAN overcome!*

Common Viewpoints Concerning

Depression Shared by Mental Health Experts

I. The causes of depression are not fully known; however, it is most likely a combination of genetic and biological factors, medical causes, as well as life styles and environmental factors. Using the information I have gathered, let's break these down in an effort to gain an understanding about what each one means:

A. **Genetic and Biological:** Some types of depression tend to run in families, suggesting a genetic link; however, depression can occur in people without family histories of depression. Researchers have been able to determine that to some degree depressive illnesses can be inherited. What appears to be inherited is a susceptibility (or vulnerability) toward depression. What does this mean? If we have a close family member that has been diagnosed as clinically depressed, we may inherit a tendency to develop the illness. *It does not mean that we are destined to become depressed.*

B. **Medical Causes:** Diseases that affect the brain, such as Parkinson's, Multiple Sclerosis, and Alzheimer's can cause depression due to the disease process. Health problems that cause chronic pain or disability can also trigger depression. The risk of depression is highest when the physical problems cause major changes to someone's lifestyle. Depression is often common in diseases that affect the immune system or the body's hormones. Hypothyroidism, (a condition caused by low levels of thyroid hormone) commonly contributes to depressed moods and fatigue. Hormonal imbalances of any kind can bring about depression.

C. **Lifestyle Factors:** The three major lifestyle factors usually common in those diagnosed with depression are lack of exercise, poor diet, and substance abuse.

1. *Lack of exercise:* Exercise has been proven to be a critical key in fighting depression. Studies show that exercise is not only a huge mood booster but is as effective, if not more so, than antidepressant treatment! Researchers have found that exercising as little as three times a week can lift the symptoms of depression, and daily walks of thirty minutes (or more) are even more effective.

2. *Poor diet:* Poor eating habits can wreak havoc on your mood, not to mention your body. Junk food and sugary snacks can cause rapid changes in blood sugar, resulting in a temporary "high" followed by "crash and burn." The same is true of caffeinated beverages. And if you aren't eating enough complex carbohydrates, produce, and lean protein, you probably aren't getting enough of the nutrients your mind and body need. I know this isn't fun to hear, but if we desire a healthy mind and body then we must change our ways and educate ourselves!

3. *Substance abuse:* Some people abuse alcohol and drugs in an effort to self-medicate and ease their symptoms of depression; however, it is now believed that substance abuse itself causes depression. Alcohol is particularly dangerous because it acts as a depressant that slows down brain activity. Another problem is the use of marijuana.

It has been proven that excessive use can also lead to depression. What about "uppers," such as amphetamines and cocaine? They initially stimulate the nervous system but when the effect wears off depression usually follows. None of these options are healthy choices!

D. **Environmental Factors**: Life stressors, such as: relationship problems, financial difficulties, death of a loved one, or medical illness can cause depression to manifest. Environmental factors encompass actual physical surroundings, as well as cultural or social background situations.

II. Thinking is always involved, and is a common pathway to depression. The good news is that you CAN control your thinking! You can choose what you allow your mind to dwell and focus on. Learning to control your *thought life* or what some experts call, *pathway of thinking,* is a powerful aid in controlling the onset of depression.

III. There is no one answer for what causes depression, yet there appears to be at least four pathways to depression: physiology, stress, learning, and thinking.

A. **Physiology:** This is simply the study of the function of living things, including processes such as nutrition, movement, and reproduction. Webster's dictionary tells us it is: "a specific response by the body to a stimulus, as fear or pain that disturbs or interferes with the normal physiological equilibrium of an organism." An example of this can be a lack of energy due to being overweight, which can ultimately lead to depression. If we change our eating habits and gain an understanding about why we overeat, we can lose weight, get healthy and feel better about ourselves!

B. **Stress:** At some point in our life we all come to know what stress is, even children. They may not understand their problem is stress related; however, when stress happens they will react to it in some way. Emotions go haywire, tempers flare, or some people shut down and keep things bottled up inside. (I am not one of those people, although I am sure my husband and family wishes I'd give it a try!) A simple definition for stress from Webster's dictionary is this: "The action on a body of any system of balanced forces whereby strain or deformation results."

C. **Learning**: Learning is where we gain knowledge, acquire experience or an ability or skill to become aware or informed. Throughout our lifetime we are continuously learning, and we are never too old to learn something new or a better way of dealing with life and emotions. *Choices. It is all about choices!*

D. **Thinking:** Studies have proven we *can* control what we choose to dwell and focus on. Changing our *thought life* is vital to conquering depression! Thinking is where we reason, analyze, invent, or conceive something. It is a belief or opinion, such as, "I think so." In thinking we have a conscious mind to form beliefs, opinions, etc., which means, *we can* control our thoughts.

Now that we have read what mental health experts agree on in regards to depression, let's look at God's Word for help on how to break free. As we go through this devotion, get ready to receive truth into your heart and make a decision to apply it to your life. A miracle of deliverance is waiting for you. Laura chose well and chose life. You can do the same!

Depression is living under the curse, and Jesus has redeemed us from the curse through His death and resurrection. Settle it in your mind today that depression is not something God has conjured up to humble us or teach us a lesson. That is not part of our Heavenly Father's character. Because your body is the Temple of the Lord, and you belong to Jesus Christ, depression has absolutely no right to you. Every part of you belongs to God, including your mind. Now is the time for you to take back your mind and body!

To understand more about blessings and curses read Deuteronomy Chapter 28. You will discover the blessings that come from obedience and the curses reaped from disobedience; however, keep in mind we are redeemed from the curse through the precious blood of Christ. In the name of Jesus, we have the right to be set free, healed, restored, and abundantly blessed!

"Christ purchased our freedom [redeeming us] from the curse (doom) of the Law [and its condemnation] by [Himself] becoming a curse for us, for it is written [in the Scriptures], cursed is everyone who hangs on a tree (is crucified); To the end that through [their receiving] Christ Jesus, the blessing [promised] to Abraham might come upon the Gentiles, so that we through faith might [all] receive [the realization of] the promise of the [Holy] Spirit." (Galatians 3:13-14, AMP)

The Word tells us *through faith* the blessings promised to Abraham are for us as well. So what about Abraham? He was a man blessed by God, *not because of works but because of his faith!* Faith is crucial in our walk with God. Romans 14:23 states, "and everything that does not come from faith is sin."

If Abraham's good deeds made him acceptable to God, he would have had something to boast about. But that was not God's way. For the Scriptures tell us, 'Abraham believed God, and God counted him as righteous because of his faith.'

When people work, their wages are not a gift, but something they have earned. *But people are counted as righteous, not because of their work, but because of their faith in God who forgives sinners."* (Romans 4:2-5, NLT, emphasis added)

To sum it up, anyone who puts their faith in Jesus Christ through the gift of salvation, has the right to seek after and receive the blessings of God. *By faith*, we can daily walk in those blessings. There is hope, there is healing, and there truly is bondage-breaking deliverance!

IV. **Depression is a spiritual battle!** The Bible says, "Be not grieved and depressed, for the joy of the Lord is your strength and stronghold." (Nehemiah 8:10, AMP) If the enemy can't snuff out our life, he will do whatever he can in an attempt to kill, steal, or destroy our joy. You see, if he takes our joy he can successfully rob us of a fruitful and happy life. He desperately wants to keep us from living a victorious existence by consuming our mind with thoughts of pain, despair, and anything negative and destructive.

Think about it. The enemy wants to steal our destiny. He longs to destroy our Christian testimony and the hope of living a powerful, overcoming life. There is no greater joy than to serve God and minister to others about the love of Jesus, but to be effective our life must reflect the blessings of God or our words mean nothing. When someone is suffering with depression he or she may be living and breathing, but that individual does not feel truly alive. One of Laura's statements perfectly describes this debilitating fact when she said, "I felt invisible, as though I barely existed; however, I watched other people living their lives."

Make no mistake about it, this is war! Can we win this battle? Absolutely! We must remember what the Bible tells us, "You are from God, little children, and have overcome them; because greater is He who is in you than he who is in the world." (1 John 4:4, ISV). We have a promise from Jesus Christ that you will read throughout this Devotional; "I can do all things through Christ which strengtheneth me." (Philippians 4:13, KJV) There is no battle too hard for God. He can do anything *but* fail, and He longs to bring healing to your mind, soul, and body!

In closing, remember what Laura said at the end of her story and make a decision to put this into practice in your own life. First, don't give up. Choose to believe God not only has the power to heal, but He wants to heal you. Second, even in the hard times praise God and speak His truth...*out loud.* Even when you don't feel like it, continuously recite Bible verses pertaining to deliverance. Sing and praise God, *in advance* and *by faith.* Third, learn the importance of aligning yourself with God's truth *every day.* Realize you have a choice in the matter. *Choose Christ and His truths for your life.*

Stop agreeing with the enemy and start believing in the all-powerful God of Heaven and earth. He is our Creator and the Maker of *all* things. Dive into God's Holy Word and find out what He says about our past, present, and future. His forgiveness is immeasurable, His mercy is incomprehensible, and His love is all consuming!

You are God's child and the enemy does not have any right to your life unless you allow him access. We give him permission with our words; which is why the Bible tells us the tongue has the power to speak life or death. In other words, watch your mouth! Discover truth by reading

God's Word, then speak His truth not the enemy's lies. When you begin consistently doing this, *God will bring forth a miracle in your life!*

"The tongue has the power of life and death, and those who love it will eat its fruit." (Proverbs 18:21, NIV)

Laura's graduation from Bethany College

Chapter 7

Lessons from Furniture

"What if some did not have faith? Will their lack of faith nullify God's faithfulness? Not at all! Let God be true, and every man a liar." (Romans 3: 3-4, NIV)

Scripture Focus

"But He was pierced for our transgressions, He was crushed for our iniquities; the punishment that brought us peace was upon Him, *and by His stripes we are healed."* (Isaiah 53:5, NIV, emphasis added)

"...by His wounds *you have been* healed." (1 Peter 2:24, NIV, emphasis added)

"This *righteousness* from God comes *through faith* in Jesus Christ to *all* who believe. *There is no difference,* for all have sinned and fall short of the glory of God, and are *justified* freely *by His grace* through the *redemption* that came *by Christ Jesus.* God presented Him as a *sacrifice of atonement, through faith in His blood."* (Romans 3:22-25a, NIV, emphasis added)

Dreams of Furniture

By Dr. Donna Wilcox

God can speak to us in many different ways, and it is wise not to put Him in a box and limit His ability to speak however He pleases. I love the story in Numbers 22, where God spoke through a donkey! It is very interesting, and I highly recommend that you take some time and read it for yourself. Below are a few scriptures from Numbers you may find intriguing and will ignite a desire to study this story.

"When the donkey saw the angel of the LORD, she lay down under Balaam; so Balaam was angry and struck the donkey with his stick. And the LORD opened the mouth of the donkey, and she said to Balaam, "What have I done to you, that you have struck me these three times?" Then Balaam said to the donkey, "Because you have made a mockery of me! If there had been a sword in my hand, I would have killed you by now." The donkey said to Balaam, "Am I not your donkey on which you have ridden all your life to this day? Have I ever been accustomed to do so to you?" And he said, "No." Then the LORD opened the eyes of Balaam, and he saw the angel of the LORD standing in the way with his drawn sword in his hand; and he bowed [h]all the way to the ground." (Numbers 22:27-31, NIV)

God is our Creator and He knows just the right way to get our attention. He used dreams about furniture to teach me some valuable lessons on healing and standing as the righteousness of Christ. I would like to share these lessons with you in the hope they will shed some important Biblical truths on the mercy and unconditional love our Father has for *all* His children.

In my autobiography, *Falling into Faith,* I detailed many obstacles and challenges I faced due to sickness, but because of God's grace and mercy I miraculously and victoriously overcame them all! Although I'm left with scars, I am thankful for every one of them. They are a constant reminder of God's healing power and tender mercies.

One obstacle in particular sent me on a new journey with God as I began growing my faith as never before. After being diagnosed with a rare form of soft tissue sarcoma, I found myself in a state of desperation. I started to hunger not only for healing, but also a deeper and more intimate relationship with the Father; however, I suffered with some major insecurities. You see, I did not feel worthy to ask for healing. And the idea of standing as the righteousness of Christ, one who is fully covered by His blood without the shame of my past and all its failures constantly lurking in the shadows, definitely felt impossible. God knew this, and He understood the importance of getting the truth of His love and mercy inside my heart and mind. This is where furniture comes into the story!

Allow me to back up in time for just a moment and explain why furniture probably consumed my thoughts during this season of my life. Not long after Bob and I got married we purchased our first living room suite together. A few months later we decided to buy new bedroom furniture. Both times I enjoyed the best shopping experiences of my life. What made them so enjoyable was the fact we paid cash and could actually afford to purchase exactly what we wanted. It felt great! No monthly bills, no added interest to pay, and no eating peanut butter and jelly for months on end because of debt. I felt rich! God knows everything about us, and He knew the lasting and positive impact these experiences etched upon my heart and mind.

After my diagnosis, a typical day consisted of reading scriptures and begging God for mercy and healing. My cancer was so rare doctors were limited in treating it. Without a miracle, life as I knew it would cease to exist! At the end of each day, I fell into bed ready for sleep. I welcomed sleep, because it was the only thing that separated me from another day of once again begging God for undeserved mercy.

As I lay sleeping one night, I began to dream. In my dream, Bob and I walked into a huge furniture store. We found everything we wanted and Bob pulled out his wallet and gave the man cash. The clerk gave us a receipt, and we left the store. Hand in hand we strolled to the car, excited about our new purchase.

The next thing I saw, we were pulling in our driveway and going inside the house. As I entered the front door, I heard God speak to me in a clear and powerful voice. He asked me a question, "Donna is the furniture you just bought yours?"

I quickly replied, "Yes, it's all ours!"

God then said, "Why do you say it is yours? It is not in your house; it is still in the store."

Without hesitation I responded, "We gave the man cash; it is paid in full, and we have the receipt. We are just waiting for delivery!"

As soon as I heard myself utter those words I awoke to hear the voice of God say, "Donna, healing is already yours; it has been paid for by the blood of Jesus. Just like the furniture in your dream, you are simply waiting for it to be delivered. Not all of My miracles are instantaneous!"

Waking up from something like this is quite incredible. I lay there weeping as the love of God ran through every cell of my being. Bob woke up and I began sharing the details of my dream and the words God spoke to me. I exploded with excitement as I confessed and acknowledged healing was mine and paid in full by Jesus on the cross. Just because it did not happen the very moment I prayed, did not mean God said "no" or that I wasn't going to receive it. We both wept and praised God for His message of love and mercy.

It is amazing how simple the revelation of healing became to me in that moment. All the confusion and overwhelming compulsion to repeatedly beg God for undeserved mercy, just disappeared. I could never deserve this amazing gift, but He did it for me anyway. He did it for each and every one of us. God's beautiful act of unconditional love has been paid in full. The gift of healing is part of the salvation plan, and is free to *all* who believe and by faith *calls things that are not as though they were.* What a loving, generous, and powerful Savior!

"As it is written: "I have made you a father of many nations." He is our father in the sight of God, in whom he believed--*the God who gives life to the dead and calls things that are not as though they were.*" (Romans 4:17, NIV, emphasis added).

The pain Jesus bore and the blood He shed on the cross was not only for our salvation but for healing too. During my studies of the Bible in Hebrew and Greek, I was overcome with gratitude to discover the very word *salvation* includes everything we could ever need or want in life. The truth of God's Word is liberating and exciting!

This turned out to be just the beginning of several lessons I learned from furniture. You see, I still struggled with another problem which continued to have an impact on my prayer life. I felt so beat down and unworthy of God's blessings. In fact, when good things happened I often thought, "I know I don't deserve this; something bad will probably happen soon. I just don't see how God can look past all my mess ups and still want to bless my life. I will just enjoy these blessings while I can, and pray for strength when the hammer comes down!"

To embrace these kinds of thoughts meant I obviously possessed a twisted and awful image of Father God and His loving character. I desperately needed a new and accurate revelation of His love and mercy. Truth would soon arrive in the form of another dream—about furniture!

A little more than a month passed, and every day I felt a spirit of confirmation concerning God's power and desire to completely heal my body. Physically things were miraculously improving, and yet I continued to struggle with insecurities and feelings of worthlessness. In fact, this became a daily (sometimes hourly) struggle. I soon realized the enemy did not want me to accept healing as he began targeting my weakest area—my mind!

God knows everything, and He knew my struggle with insecurities and mistakes from the past. I felt incapable of shaking them off and feeling any sense of value. He waited for me to get completely quiet and sound asleep, and then He visited my dreams once again in a magnificent way. I truly feel God has to speak to a lot of us in our sleep. It is probably the only time He can get us to shut up and listen! At least that seems to be the case with me.

There I lay, sound asleep, and once again dreaming about furniture. This time I dreamed my dad came to see me with a wonderful surprise. Keeping every aspect of my personality in mind, he bought the most exquisite bedroom suite I had ever seen. It was painstakingly and intricately designed down to every precise detail, and made just for me, his daughter.

The mattress had been strategically created so that I would wake up every day feeling rested and refreshed. The inside of each dresser drawer was lined with the fragrance of my favorite perfume. I could not believe my father's generosity and the time it must have taken him to pick everything out, making sure it was perfect down to the smallest detail.

I gave him a great big hug but expressed how much I did not deserve this lavish gift. He beamed with excitement and proclaimed, "I want you to have it to show you how much I love you!" He gave me another hug and left, leaving behind the bedroom suite for me to enjoy as a reminder of his love for me—his daughter.

Several days passed, and I heard a knock on the door. When I opened the door, there stood my dad smiling from ear to ear. He anxiously stepped inside and went straight to the bedroom. He began to ask, "How does the bed sleep? Do your clothes smell like your favorite perfume every morning?" As he continued to ask questions he noticed something strange. My clothes were in a box on the floor, not in the beautifully lined and scented drawers he so meticulously picked out for me. To make matters worse, the bed with the perfect mattress looked as if it had never been slept in! He looked stunned and confused. I hung my head in shame not knowing what to say, but I knew he deserved an explanation.

Finally, I looked up at Dad as tears streamed down my face and said, "Daddy, it is just too beautiful and I don't deserve it. I cannot bring myself to sleep in that wonderful bed or put my clothes in those perfect drawers. Please forgive me, but I am just not worthy to receive such a gift."

Broken and sad he turned around and said, "Baby, I did all this just for you. I did not ask you to be worthy, I just wanted to express the depths of my love." As his eyes filled with tears, he walked out the door.

Once again, I awoke to God's voice as He said something incomprehensible: "Donna, when I see you I see red, the blood of Jesus. I see My daughter, one that I love. Take this gift and learn to stand as the righteousness of Christ. Do not live in shame or disgrace because of the past. I have forgiven you and put a new song of joy in your heart. Receive this gift so others will see My love and realize I long for them to walk in freedom too. Be a light of truth in the midst of the darkness!"

You see, in my dream I could not bring myself to enjoy this awesome gift of love. And because of my inability to receive, Dad walked away sad and hurt. He just wanted to express his love for me. Not because I did anything special or deserved it, and not because I never made mistakes. He simply wanted to say, "Daughter, I love you!"

God used this dream to show me just how much He loves His children and demonstrated that love by sending His Son as a sacrifice for our sins. When Jesus died and rose again He brought forgiveness, healing, and the ability to stand clean before Him through the cleansing power of His blood. When He sees His precious ones, He truly sees the blood of the

Lamb; not our shortcomings or failures. No one is worthy of such an act of love, but He did it for us anyway! How could I continue to hurt His heart and not receive this gift?

As I lay there in a puddle of tears, the all-consuming love of God covered me like a blanket. As my heart overflowed with joy, I once again woke Bob up and shared this new revelation of God's love. The moment I began sharing my dream with Bob something happened I did not expect—a holy boldness! I have never felt such determination to shake off the past. No longer would I allow my vision to be blinded and unable to see God's love and mercy. I felt free, loved, and so thankful to be a daughter of the Most High God!

This new revelation sent me down a brand new path of freedom and liberty with my Savior. By catching a glimpse into a love I will never fully understand or deserve, I began learning how to walk in the light of His truth without bondage and condemnation. This all-consuming love allowed me the freedom to grow in my relationship with Christ and live every day full of praise and gratitude to be a recipient of its life changing power!

~The End~

Truth

It is one thing to possess book knowledge, but something altogether different to receive an understanding or revelation about what you are reading and studying! Having been a student of God's Word since childhood, I knew the scripture clearly states in Isaiah 64:6, *all our righteous acts are like filthy rags.* The option to work our way into Heaven is nonexistent. Truly understanding what this meant, and getting it from my head into my heart made an incredible difference!

You see, there is absolutely nothing any of us can ever do or accomplish that will make us a worthy or acceptable recipient of God's love and mercy. This brings true equality and justice to the gift of salvation for everyone. God's requirement for receiving this precious gift is to acknowledge Jesus Christ is the Son of God, with a repentant heart seek forgiveness for our sins, and make Jesus the Lord and Savior of our life. Once we are saved, *by faith* we begin the process of *working out our salvation in fear and trembling.*

"So then, my beloved, just as you have always obeyed, not as in my presence only, but now much more in my absence, work out your salvation with fear and trembling; for it is God who is at work in you, both to will and to work for His good pleasure." (Philippians 2:12-13, NASB)

"Know that a man is not justified by observing the law, but *by faith* in Jesus Christ. So we, too, have put our faith in Christ Jesus that we may be justified *by faith* in Christ and not by observing the law, because by observing the law no one will be justified." (Galatians 2:16, NIV, emphasis added)

What does it mean to *work out our salvation in fear and trembling*? When people hear the word, "fear," they usually think in negative terms, such as being afraid, anxiety, alarm, or dread. I want to explain what the word, "fear," means in this text, because our Heavenly Father does not operate on the principles of fear. He is a God of faith.

When we accept Jesus Christ as our Savior we are to walk in the *fear of the Lord.* Below is a definition Bob and I learned during our days in missionary school. It truly spoke to our hearts and brought clarity and understanding. I pray it will do the same for you.

Strong's Dictionary: The fear of the Lord is *"Reverential fear* of God, as a controlling motive of life, in matters spiritual and moral, *not a mere fear of His power and righteous retribution, but a wholesome dread of displeasing Him.* A fear which banishes the terror that shrinks from His presence."

When we walk in the fear of the Lord, we will work out our salvation in a reverential fear and wholesome dread of displeasing our loving and wonderful Savior. We will be inspired to seek wisdom about the choices we make in life, and desire to walk in love toward Father God and our fellow man.

The Bible often compares our relationship with Christ to marriage. His Word tells us the *Lord delights over us as a bridegroom rejoices over his bride;* and Jesus Christ (our Bridegroom) will one day return for His children—His beloved bride!

When I think about this comparison it causes me to reflect on my wedding day. I cannot ever remember feeling so many emotions at one time. It was incredibly scary, yet wonderful. When Bob and I left for the chapel to get married, I literally shook so much I felt like one of those big jack hammers! Why? Was I terrified of Bob, and did I dread the idea of marrying him? No! I trembled with excitement from the love I felt and all the expectations about our future. I also felt the weight of responsibility and sensed the importance of what was taking place. With every fiber of my being I longed to be a blessing to Bob. I desired to be a good wife, lover, and friend. I can only imagine how Bob felt. He was about to marry a woman diagnosed with a rare cancer, and without a miracle the future did not look too promising!

For just a moment, think about how much Jesus must love each and every one of us to suffer the shame and agony of the cross. Reflect back to the day you made a commitment to let Him into your heart. Something wonderful and frightening happened in that moment; a change, a glorious change! The day you welcomed Him into your life He became your Beloved Redeemer.

"I delight greatly in the LORD; my soul rejoices in my God. For he has clothed me with garments of salvation and arrayed me in a robe of righteousness, as a bridegroom adorns his head like a priest, and as a bride adorns herself with her jewels." (Isaiah 61:10, NIV)

"As a young man marries a maiden, so will your sons marry you; as a bridegroom rejoices over his bride, so will your God rejoice over you." (Isaiah 62:5, NIV)

"Let us rejoice and be glad and give him glory! For the wedding of the Lamb has come, and his bride has made herself ready." (Revelation 19:7, NIV)

When we walk in the fear of the Lord, it builds a relationship between us and our Creator which is both powerful and miraculous. As Children of God, we have the right to boldly approach the throne of grace and make our petitions known to our Heavenly Father. In turn, our lives will produce a harvest of blessings and become a testimony for all to see!

Becoming a Christian does not mean we will never make mistakes or we can somehow work hard enough to deserve what Christ did for us on the cross. We will never be good or saintly enough to merit His beautiful gift of unconditional love and mercy. It also does not mean we can sloppily live our lives in a destructive way, expecting God's mercy and grace to come to our rescue and cover our sins when we are not truly repentant to begin with!

Yes, if with a truly repentant heart we ask for forgiveness, God will forgive. However, true repentance means to turn from the path of disobedience and walk the straight and narrow. In other words: *walk in the fear of the Lord.* The precious blood of Jesus is not a free ticket for us to continue sinning and expect blessings and favor to overtake us! The following scriptures bring clarity and truth concerning the attitudes and actions of a true Believer.

"No one who is born of God will continue to sin, because God's seed remains in him; he cannot go on sinning, because he has been born of God. *This is how we know who the Children of God are and who the children of the devil are: Anyone who does not do what is right is not a Child of God; nor is anyone who does not love his brother.*" (1 John 3:9-10, NIV, emphasis added)

I pray these lessons from furniture have given you a glimpse into the mercy and love God has for us, along with the blessings that come from being His child. It is hard to imagine a love this pure and unconditional, but it is real and it is for *all* who are willing to believe and receive!

I have been cancer free for over 18 years and it truly is a miracle! Chemotherapy does not work on this form of soft-tissue sarcoma; however, radiation has been successful in prolonging recurrences. The problem with this particular cancer is the frequent recurrences and how quickly it penetrates through. Without warning, a tumor could grow anywhere in your body and you would not even be aware of it. The tumor, (along with all the tissue and nerves it has touched), must be removed within a certain timeframe; nothing else can be done other than radiation. After seeking God for wisdom and doing a lot of research, I declined radiation. I do not have a spleen, which means it is difficult to fight off infection. I simply was not at peace with the amount of radiation doctors recommended. Bob and I sought God and trusted Him to carry us through to victory, and He did just that!

Every year I receive several letters and calls from the tumor registry and medical researchers asking if I am still among the living, along with a number of other questions. This continues to open the door to testify about God's healing power! So you see, Jesus Christ is still in the miracle-working business, and His plans for us will be fulfilled if we make a choice to hold on to His Word and trust in His power to bring it to pass.

I often wondered why God healed me but not my mother. The only thing that makes sense is the fact mom trusted God to take her home when He was ready. Mom knew she was not going anywhere until she accomplished everything God called her to do. Throughout her life, mom served the Lord with all her heart. As a Chaplain and Counselor, I have seen and experienced many things I cannot explain or understand, but at the end of the day I can say with complete peace and assurance, "I trust God and His wisdom in ALL things!"

Starting today speak God's truth over your life. Stop allowing the enemy to consume your mind with guilt and condemnation over your past or anything else. You are a child of God, and the precious blood of the Lamb covers your sins. You are gloriously and amazingly forgiven!

In closing, I want to leave you with a few Greek definitions of three words: *Atonement, Righteousness*, and *Justification*. Take time to read Romans, chapters 3 and 4. As you read and study, keep these definitions in mind and meditate on the scriptures.

Some of our kids have a saying when they are describing something amazing: "It will rock your world!" Trust me, it most definitely will!

1. *Atonement: Our wrath taker; hilasterion—meaning; an overflowing, overwhelming, out-of-control love!*
2. *Righteousness: Perfectly measured up to God's standard or right standing with God.*
3. *Justification: A declaration that a person is righteous.*

"The fear of the LORD is the beginning of knowledge, But fools despise wisdom and instruction." (Proverbs 1:7, NKJV)

Chapter 8

A Tenacious, Loving God

"I waited patiently for the Lord; He turned to me and heard my cry. He lifted me out of the slimy pit, out of the mud and mire; He set my feet on a rock and gave me a firm place to stand. He put a new song in my mouth, a hymn of praise to our God. Many will see and fear and put their trust in the Lord. Blessed is the man who makes the Lord His trust." (Psalm 40:1-4, NIV)

Scripture Focus

"Praise the Lord, O my soul; all my inmost being, praise His holy name. Praise the Lord, O my soul, and forget not all His benefits, who forgives all your sins and heals all your diseases, who redeems your life from the pit and crowns you with love and compassion, who satisfies your desires with good things so that your youth is renewed like the eagle's. The Lord works righteousness and justice for all the oppressed." (Psalm 103:1-6, NIV)

Released from Prison

By Danika Potter

I am left speechless by the tenacity of God. Believers I have met usually have a story, tailored especially to them, of how God captured their heart, how He relentlessly pursued them with His love, until the person had nowhere else to run but straight into His arms. I met a woman that our loving God pursued in such a manner, and although I knew her for only a short amount of time, her story resonates in my heart.

This woman lives in a fundamentalist, war-torn, Islamic nation. She grew up under the oppression not only of outside invaders and power-hungry militants but also under a religious system that said her purpose in life was not much more than to be a servant. According to this depressed system, her accepted roles included cooking, cleaning, satisfying a man, and having babies, preferably male ones. Other than that, she had no reason to exist.

Her marriage was arranged according to her culture and tradition, and she was promised to a much older man. There was no joy, no girlish giddiness or dreams of white dresses and hopes of a happy marriage; it was merely her duty.

When it seemed her life could not get any more hopeless, disaster struck. On her wedding day, two relatives kidnapped her and took her hundreds of miles from her own home to the capital city in order to sell her as a prostitute. Only then did a duty-filled marriage to an old man seem like paradise in comparison with what was happening. As the men were on their way to sell her, they were intercepted by the local authorities and taken into custody. The men told their story, the woman hers, and then came the verdict: the men could go free, and the woman was to go to prison because of her "indiscretion." Her accusers viewed her as dirty, charging her with allowing the men to sell her as a prostitute and willingly giving herself away. A woman's honor is usually encapsulated in her virginity and is to be protected above all other things in her culture, and yet it is the one thing that is most marred by gossip and accusation.

Soon this woman found herself in a prison hundreds of miles away from family. Her honor had been tarnished for the rest of her life. Regardless of the truth, she would be forever labeled and shunned with no promise of a future and most probably never marry. Before long she received news that the man she was engaged to had married her sister. The future was bleak, hopeless. She slipped further and further into despondency. Day after day she sat in a crowded room full of women accused of stealing, some falsely accused of crimes, and others who had killed their husbands. In desperation, they saw this as the only release from the personal prison of their lives, finding more freedom in their current physical captivity.

Even if this woman were to get out of prison, she had no place to go. Her own family would not take her back, and no man would want her as a wife. Prison was the only place she had to lay her head, the only place to call home.

Throughout this process of pain and despair, Jesus, the Bridegroom, the Lover of her soul was wooing this precious woman into His arms. He sent a group of foreign missionaries into that prison, and they not only cleaned and freshened up the physical prison cell, but also shared the story of a man who extends an invitation of redemption and love and could release them from the prison in their hearts and their painful devastation. This young woman, in her twenties and weary from life, had suffered more than most will ever suffer, but that day she met Jesus. In a stuffy, smelly prison cell, she found the Love of her life and eternal freedom. Oh, the tenacious, passionate love of our God!

As we knelt with this woman, shared tears, and prayed together, the Holy Spirit wrapped His arms around all of us. In that moment, He whispered of a love so intimate, so passionate, and so complete that we could not help but give our lives in worship to Him. That day in a dirty, dark prison cell, the shepherd picked up the 100th sheep and gently carried it into His fold, saying, "You're home now, little one. Don't fear; you're home."

Today, this woman has been released and is living with relatives who have miraculously received her into their home. She is sharing with others the love and freedom she has found in Jesus, her Friend and Redeemer!

~The End~

Truth

Danika is a beautiful young woman, and just happens to be one of the "spiritual daughters" the Lord has brought into our family. She has blessed our lives, and we are so proud of her willing heart to spread the Gospel in a very difficult place.

As you read this chapter, please take a moment and pray for those serving God in dangerous, faraway places. Ask the Lord to protect and anoint their lives with the grace to walk the road they have chosen with peace, integrity, and courage. God loves intercessory prayer and He is faithful to answer. Your prayers could very well open the door to the miraculous as they persevere in their mission.

Reading Danika's story reminded me of so many precious women we met in Mexico and India. Their beautiful faces revealed a life of pain and suffering. Many of us will never experience the devastation they have endured, and we must be mindful of our Christian calling to pray for the oppressed. Prayer changes things!

God's love can reach past the hurt, past the lonely, and into the darkest places on earth. He longs to reach the lost with the message of hope. For He truly is a tenacious, loving Father! His desire is that no one perish but all come to the knowledge of His Saving Grace.

Because of the fall of man there is sin, pain, and tribulation in this world; however, we have the key to an amazing and overwhelming love that supplies us with the strength to walk through anything. We also have the promise of a home in Heaven when our time on earth is complete. What joy and peace this knowledge brings, especially to those who are hurting. They long for the hope of a better tomorrow. When they leave this world they can go to the arms of a loving and faithful Father; where there is no more pain or tears. They will be greeted with unconditional love and complete acceptance. This revelation of God's love brings enormous comfort to a troubled spirit, hurting body, and confused mind.

I want to encourage you to regularly pray and intercede for others who are suffering in ways most of us will never experience. Pray for the missionaries and pastors desperately trying to reach them. Pray for the love of God and the message of hope to miraculously penetrate the darkness. Pray for people to rise up and answer the call to go to these hard places, and with unwavering faith prepare to *give all* for the sake of Christ!

As Ambassadors of Christ, be willing to ask this question; "What is God's will for my life concerning missions?" It is never too late! You may find God is leading you to become a missionary in a faraway land or in your own neighborhood. Perhaps you will answer the call to faithfully intercede on behalf of others. The Lord may speak to your heart about financially supporting a ministry or mission that is reaching the lost in a dangerous and difficult location. Missions is not about geography. Where-ever people are lost and hurting is a mission field that is dear to the heart of God. We all have a part and no one who says they are a Christian is exempt. Ask, listen, and obey! Prayer is powerful and as Believers we must do it with conviction. Become purposeful and tenacious!

Whatever God calls you to do, *be faithful*. Having been a missionary, I want to urge you to honor your commitments. Whether a missionary is in another country or serving in the United States, a one-time pledge or even ten dollars a month can be a huge blessing.

In Danika's story she referred to the "Parable of the Lost Sheep." In closing, I want to reflect on this parable because it beautifully describes the purpose for which we, as Believers, are called. There is no greater joy than to witness the moment someone accepts Jesus as their Lord and Savior. Equally important is the privilege of bringing someone who has lost their way back into the fold, returning them to the Father's arms of love!

"Then Jesus told them this parable. 'Suppose one of you has a hundred sheep and loses one of them. Does he not leave the ninety-nine in the open country and go after the lost sheep until he finds it? And when he finds it, he joyfully puts it on his shoulders and goes home. Then he calls his friends and neighbors together and says, 'Rejoice with me; I have found my lost sheep.' I tell you that in the same way there will be more rejoicing in heaven over one sinner who repents than over ninety-nine righteous persons who do not need to repent." (Luke 15:3-7, NIV)

If you would like to know more about Danika's ministry and others like her, please contact me through my website; http://www.donnawilcox.com. These young people are amazing and giving to their ministry is sowing into good seed!

Danika

Chapter 9

How to Get Your Prayers Answered!

"If ye abide in Me, and My words abide in you, ye shall ask what ye will, and it shall be done unto you." (John 15:7, KJV)

Scripture Focus

"And call upon Me, and I will answer him. (Psalm 91:15, KJV)

"Evening, and morning, and at noon, will I pray, and cry aloud; and He shall hear my voice." (Psalm 55:17, KJV)

"I tell you the truth, My Father will give you whatever you ask in My name. Until now you have not asked for anything in My name. Ask and you will receive, and your joy will be complete." (John 16:23, 24, NIV)

"If ye then, being evil, know how to give good gifts unto your children, how much more shall your Father which is in heaven give good things to them that ask Him? (Matthew 7:11, KJV)

A God Story

By: Scott and Cathie Homan, Missionaries

A complete stranger gave us a car today, and we are busting at the seams to share this miracle with everyone! It was not just any car, either. It just happened to be a car we wanted to purchase, an Audi wagon.

For some time we had been saving money and praying for a reliable car to replace our Honda. For several months we looked high and low, praying for God to show us just the right one. We got close to making a few offers, but nothing felt completely right. One day I told Scott, "I want a God story with this." We always read about these things and heard about other people's stories, but we wanted to witness one for ourselves. At times it seemed discouraging, but Scott remained steady, knowing God was going to come through, and of course, He did!

Over the weekend Scott saw a 1994, pearly white Audi wagon for sale. It had all the things we wanted in a car; all-wheel drive, leather seats, power everything, big enough for a car seat (for our little one that could arrive just any day) and it was $4,500! We called the guy and arranged to take it for a test drive, and we really liked it. Afterwards we sat talking with the family and found out they were Christians. They also knew of YWAM, so we felt a bit of a connection with them.

When we got home Scott and I prayed whether we were to make an offer on the car or not. We both felt peace about it and did not have any *checks* in our spirits. We were excited! We felt like we were to offer $3,800 for it. We knew if they accepted that offer it would have to be God because the blue book value was $4,800! Scott made the offer, and they accepted it without hesitation. We went to the bank and got out $3,800 and met with the couple to buy the car. When we got to their home, they continued to ask about YWAM and what we do. They seemed very interested, and we were happy to tell them about our mission's work!

As the man handed the title over to us, he said these words: "Well, when we were praying about this car, we really felt like God wanted us to just give it to you." Immediately, tears began filling my eyes as Scott tried to argue with them. It felt like a dream, and I could not comprehend what was happening. Then his wife said, "There is no argument here. This is a gift from God, and we're just doing what He wants us to do!" Then she proceeded to tell us how they came to this decision. Two weeks prior to putting their car on the market their pastor began sharing about giving away possessions, and continued to talk about it each week. He said how he loved to give away cars. The wife (who gave us the car) shared how she felt that seemed so irresponsible, and she could never do that, because then they could not afford to buy their current car if they did not make any money on this one. You see, this car had been her baby. They paid $18,000 for it in 2001, and it was not something they just wanted to give away.

The previous Sunday they went away together for their anniversary, and she told her husband, "You know, I think I could give away our car if that's what God was asking us to do. I feel in my heart I'm ready to do that." In that same weekend, Scott happened to call them to set up a time to see the car. They told us we were the only people that had asked to see their car in the two weeks it had been advertised. They prayed the night before we came and said they knew we were the exact people God wanted them to give it to! The wife referred to the woman in the Bible with only the two mites, and how it must have seemed irresponsible to others because it was all she had, yet she gave it any way. This dear lady felt God was asking her to *seem* irresponsible and give her "two mites" in this car to us! They told us it wasn't their car to give but God's, and He wanted them to give it to us.

I was completely and utterly overwhelmed. I do not think I stopped crying for a good hour. We did not even know how to properly thank them, so we just sat there speechless and then prayed for them. *We knew that we knew that we knew* this was the God story we asked for! I have not sensed God's presence over me in this capacity for so long. I felt shaken by His overwhelming love for us, even when we do not deserve it. Do we ever deserve His goodness? But isn't it His kindness that leads to repentance? It is! How many times do we think we need a good beating or a good correction? Instead, God comes in and just loves on us, and in that love our hearts cannot do anything but turn toward Him.

This situation has helped me realize that I have a lot to learn from my Heavenly Father! His kindness continuously brings me to Him. I have done *nothing* for Him that is of my own, really. I even get angry with Him sometimes when it is not even His fault, and yet He spoke directly to us. He loves us. He sees us. He blesses us when we least deserve it. He is still faithful. He cannot deny Himself.

So there you have it. We have a beautiful Audi wagon, and it was not even given to us by anyone we knew or by someone who knew our story or our needs. It was not even someone's old, beat-up car that they no longer wanted. It is a gem, a prize, and it came straight from God. In the backseat, this wonderful couple had placed a sweet gift (two sleepers) for our soon-to-be-born baby girl. How much more could we handle?

One more thing, the timing was perfect. What if we had seen the car two weeks prior, before God had a chance to work on this lady's heart? What if we had offered money on another car a month earlier and missed this blessing? The timing of God is perfect because God is perfect. He always knows what He's doing. We can trust Him!

Now we have car and money left over. We are overwhelmed and in awe of this God we serve. Why wouldn't anyone want to be a Christian? Why wouldn't they want to know this Jesus we know? He is the kindest man I know and as Graham Cooke says, "And living for Him is the most exciting fulfilling life we could have!"

~The End~

The next testimony is from Danika. She will be familiar to you because you read another one of her stories in an earlier chapter.

In an effort to protect Danika and not put her safety in jeopardy, I have carefully left out the name of the country. Prepare to be blessed as you read about God's faithfulness and answered prayer!

Humbled by God's Provision

By: Danika Potter, Missionary

Do you ever have one of those weeks when everything that is happening seems to be God narrowing in on a lesson that He wants you to grasp with your heart? In the last three months it appeared our team/ organization's flow of finances slowed to a trickle. It became as dry as the riverbeds here in this country. Now, I am not mentioning this to guilt or tell people to give. I believe this was orchestrated by the hand of God to once again bring us back to dependence upon Him and Him alone.

My personal support dropped almost in half the last two months; our organization, whose budget is in the multiple thousands a month, received mere hundreds from project supporters. Everyone on the team was scraping to make ends meet as their support had also dropped. To complicate matters, in the middle of this we moved into a new (and may I add, beautiful and home-like) house, we were increasing our staff, had upcoming projects starting again now that spring had arrived, past bills that were unpaid, and many other little things that continued to crop up.

I was in a faith valley, not despairing but looking at the numbers and what we needed. I found myself going, "Oh God, what do we do?" Moreover, God began revealing the pride in my heart, and how this was taking a blow to my pride. Our organization was getting a reputation for not being able to pay its bills. Our staff's salaries were late, and we could only give a little at a time. I was embarrassed. More than anything, I wanted the money so *I* could regain a good reputation and once again look like a decent leader.

Well, out of the blue we received a miraculous monetary gift from a very unexpected source. My pride was knocked to its knees, and I handed over the money to our accountant with tears in my eyes, asking forgiveness from the team for my pride and lack of faith in what God had called us here to do. These weeks had been full of some of the biggest leadership lessons that I had learned in awhile. This was one of them. *I must always trust God for His provision, and not just beg and plead for my own reputation to be spared.* What is my reputation in comparison to the glory God anyways?

Now for a brief example of the upcoming events and things that God is doing with our team in reaching the people of this country.

Mini Discipleship Training School, (DTS)

Every night for the next 6 weeks (and maybe longer), we are meeting on the third floor of our office; we will have dinner together, disciple, and teach approximately ten young, new Believers (all men). We are going through the basic curriculum that is taught in YWAM's DTS schools, beginning with "The Father Heart of God," "Hearing the Voice of God," "Spiritual Warfare." It has been an intense and exciting time, as I am seeing the dreams I had for this discipleship become a reality (although I'm finding it highly ironic that most of my work in this country has been with men)! However, we need much prayer.

These men are babies in the faith. Some have been asking for money and saying that if they do not get their needs met, what is the point of being a Christian? It only makes life harder for them. They have Muslim friends asking questions that are too difficult to answer and leading them to doubt, *but they are hungry!* They are hungry for truth, and they are seeking it out, and we have the exciting privilege to be able to provide it for them and see them grow in it. I feel like one of Paul's co-workers as they saw a young church grow, and struggle, and fall in love with God.

Upcoming Conference

At the end of June, the entire YWAM staff in our area will be meeting in Thailand for its first ever conference outside of the country. This is quite an exciting time for us. I will be leaving from there to return to America to prepare for my year and a half of studies at Wheaton College directly afterwards. I am really looking forward to this as a good transition time to living back in America, as my life here is so drastically different. We have a great Member Care Staff coming to help with counseling, debriefing, and prayer. I also see this as an excellent opportunity for all of us to meet from around the country where our phones are not ringing, and no one is knocking on our doors because they need one more thing. We will all get a much-needed break.

Leadership Lessons

This has been quite the intense time for me already, and I am learning some very valuable things about leadership. I've had three fourteen-hour days in a row, and God is telling me I need to manage my time better, even in this unpredictable setting. He is asking me to enter His rest. I am also learning tons about communication and keeping short accounts with team members by not letting the little things become huge! I am learning about confrontation. I hate confrontation and usually avoid it, but often, it is what is most loving for an individual or a team. I am learning more than I have ever wanted to in how to deal with government officials and people who are trying to manipulate you. Through this, I recently realized God is truly teaching me to be as wise as a serpent and innocent as a dove.

"I am sending you out like sheep among wolves. Therefore be as shrewd as snakes and as innocent as doves." (Matthew 10:16, NIV)

I just wanted to share these things with you so that you can keep me accountable and pray for the staff, as well as our team and me. I cannot make it here without prayer and the body lifting me up to our Source of all we need. This place and these people have forever changed my life!

~The End~

Truth

I want to focus on what God's Word says concerning how to get our prayers answered. What better way to begin this lesson than with some amazing stories of encouragement and answered prayer! In addition, these stories teach some important steps regarding spiritual growth and maturity.

First, let's examine the scriptures. The Bibles clearly defines specific steps in regards to receiving answers to our prayers and experiencing miracles. God does not reserve these kinds of blessings for a chosen few. One thing is certain, once you have personally experienced one of these *God stories,* it builds your faith and strengthens your testimony.

Answered prayer often happens when we are being obedient and faithful; or due to the undeniable fact God is God and He is sovereign and merciful. Notice, I did not say that God answers our prayers because we really have our stuff together and are such good and perfect people! If studying the Bible has taught me anything, it is the importance God places on three key words: *obedience, faithfulness, and mercy.*

So how do we get our prayers answered? Let's begin our journey by reading the following scriptures. They will open our spiritual eyes as we gain a better understanding on how to pray and the benefits that follow!

"…I tell you the truth, My Father will give you whatever you ask in My name…Ask and you will receive, and your joy will be complete… In that day you will ask in My name. I am not saying that I will ask the

Father on your behalf. No, the Father Himself loves you because you have loved me and have believed that I came from God." (John 16:23-24, 26-27, NIV)

So when we pray, *pray to the Father in the name of Jesus.* You see, Jesus is sitting at the right hand of the Father making intercession for us. In other words, He is intervening, negotiating, and pleading on our behalf.

"Who then will condemn us? No one—for Christ Jesus died for us and was raised to life for us, and He is sitting in the place of honor at God's right hand, pleading for us." (Romans 8:34, NLT)

Our Savior's continuous intercession proves His love and compassion for all of His cherished ones. The blood of Christ constantly atones for our sins because even after we are saved we continually sin; therefore, He never stops interceding on our behalf, presenting the merits of His obedience and death for us. His righteousness never ceases to demand mercy instead of death, and all of this is consistent with the Father's will and according to His promises.

Our Savior gives us another reason He desires to answer the prayers of His children, "...so that our joy will be complete." Our joy cannot be complete if we are out of work, in debt, our bodies are filled with pain, or we are depressed and hurting. What kind of joy is that?

According to God's Word, the next key components to remember are *pray in faith* and *believe before we receive!* Smith Wigglesworth once said, "There is something about believing God that will cause Him to pass over a million people to get to you."

"'Have faith in God.' Jesus answered. 'I tell you the truth, if anyone says to this mountain, "Go, throw yourself into the sea,' and does not doubt in his heart but believes that what he says will happen, it will be done for him. Therefore I tell you, whatever you ask for in prayer, *believe that you have received it, and it will be yours.'"* (Mark 11:22-24, NIV, emphasis added)

Notice how the above scripture is worded. It clearly directs us to *believe we have received.* I have never found one scripture that tells us to wait until we see something happen before we believe! The instructions are clear: *do not doubt, believe it will happen, and believe that we have received.* The scripture even provides the powerful results of this kind of faith: "…and it will be yours!"

We must never lose sight of one important fact; God is *faith.* We are faith children of a faith God, and our Father works on the principles of faith. **God meets faith, not need!** Romans 14:23 conveys a powerful statement: "…and everything that does not come from faith is sin." Keeping this in mind, we can understand why 2 Corinthians 5:7 tells us, "We live by faith, not by sight.*"* Another example of *believing before receiving!*

I mentioned Smith Wigglesworth earlier and I want to share one more thing he said. Although it may be a hard word, I believe it is a true statement; "Some people are ready to give up if their prayers are not answered immediately. This proves they never believed God in the first place!"

So far we have learned what the Bible says about *how to pray* and now we must go to the next step—*forgive when we pray!* This is an important part of the process in effectively praying and seeing results. You see, prayer will not work in an unforgiving heart. We simply cannot have an effective prayer life when we have unforgiveness or bitterness toward others. Mark 11:25 says it quite plainly and leaves no room for negotiation: "And when you stand praying, if you hold anything against anyone, forgive him, so that your Father in Heaven may forgive you your sins."

We are not responsible for another person's actions or choices; however, we are responsible for our own. Do not allow seeds of unforgiveness and bitterness to hinder your prayers from being answered. It isn't worth the price you will pay! Even if you have been hurt and it was not your fault, we still must forgive so that the Father can forgive our many sins and shortcomings. I am not suggesting this is easy or even fair, but if we are obedient to the scriptures, we will seek God for strength and learn to forgive. God will bring justice to our cause; in His time and in His way.

God's Word doesn't say He is fair, but the scriptures clearly teach us He is just!

"Commit everything you do to the LORD. Trust him, and he will help you. He will make your innocence radiate like the dawn, and the justice of your cause will shine like the noonday sun. Be still in the presence of the LORD, and wait patiently for him to act. Don't worry about evil people who prosper or fret about their wicked schemes." (Psalms 37:5-7, NLT)

"For I, the LORD, love justice. I hate robbery and wrongdoing. I will faithfully reward my people for their suffering and make an everlasting covenant with them." (Isaiah 61:8, NLT)

"This is what the LORD says: "Don't let the wise boast in their wisdom, or the powerful boast in their power, or the rich boast in their riches. But those who wish to boast should boast in this alone: that they truly know me and understand that I am the LORD who demonstrates unfailing love and who brings justice and righteousness to the earth, and that I delight in these things. I, the LORD, have spoken!" (Jeremiah 9:23, 24, NLT)

Next, *depend upon the Holy Spirit*. The Holy Spirit is our Comforter, Guide, and Intercessor. When we receive Christ as our Savior the Spirit dwells within us. To understand the role of the Holy Spirit, we must research the Word of God and ask the Lord to open our ears and eyes to truth. Hope and faith sustains the Believer in our Christian walk, but the Bible also tells us we have help in our weakness; including times we simply don't know how to pray.

"In the same way, the Spirit helps us in our weakness. We do not know what we ought to pray for, but the Spirit Himself intercedes for us with groans that words cannot express. And He who searches our hearts knows the mind of the Spirit, because the Spirit intercedes for the saints in accordance with God's will." (Romans 8:26, NIV)

"Therefore He is able also to save to the uttermost (completely, perfectly, finally, and for all time and eternity) those who come to God through Him, since He is always living to make petition to God and intercede with Him and intervene for them." (Hebrews 7:25, AMP)

Now we come to the step in this process that I find most rewarding; the prayer of intercession! Just as the Holy Spirit is interceding for us, we must intercede for one another. What does this mean? With unselfish determination we take the place of someone else by standing in the gap through prayer.

When you take the place of a person through intercession, you may experience the same emotions in your own spirit they are feeling. As you pray and intercede, ask the Holy Spirit to work in their hearts to bring conviction, restoration, healing, hope, or whatever is needed. Miracles happen when this prayer principle is applied!

The last point I want to make in this process is an enormous faith builder. Visualize your prayers answered in the Spirit! You see, prayers are answered in the Spirit before they are manifested in the natural. Take time to read the story of Elisha and his servant in 2 Kings 6:8-23. These scriptures offer a greater understanding on what it means to *see with the eyes of the Spirit!*

I want to close with a story from the book of Daniel. It is a beautiful example of how prayers are answered while we are actively praying. Get ready to experience a completely new outlook on the subjects of praying and answered prayer.

"While I was speaking and praying, confessing my sin and the sin of my people Israel and making my request to the LORD my God for His holy hill, while I was still in prayer, Gabriel, the man I had seen in the earlier vision, came to me in swift flight about the time of the evening sacrifice. He instructed me and said to me, 'Daniel, I have now come to give you insight and understanding. *As soon as you began to pray, an answer was given,* which I have come to tell you, for you are highly esteemed.'" (Daniel 9:20-23, NIV)

This is a story of spiritual warfare: Darkness versus light, evil versus good, and war versus peace. I want to encourage you to read the book of Daniel. It is an amazing account of God's sovereignty and power.

Without going into details, I want to focus on something so important in verse 23; "As soon as you began to pray, an answer was given." When God's people pray, an answer is being given. Just because we may not immediately see results does not mean God did not hear or does not care. He is a faithful Father. He does hear the prayers of His children, and He does answer!

Like Daniel, when we pray in faith and are waiting for an answer, we will most likely experience spiritual warfare. Just like in Bible days, the powers of the unseen world of good and evil are at work. This is why Paul warns us in Ephesians 6 to put on the full armor of God so that we can take our stand against the enemy's schemes. When we are fully equipped for battle we have the assurance of victory. *Jesus Christ will not, has not, and cannot fail. In and Through Him we are more than conquerors!*

In review, the keys to a fruitful prayer life consist of the following important elements:

- Faith
- Believe *before* we receive
- Forgive so that our prayers can be heard and answered
- Refuse to allow doubt to take up residence in our hearts
- Intercession
- Patiently wait for the answer

"No, in all these things we are more than conquerors through Him who loved us." (Romans 8:37, NIV)

Chapter 10

May I Never Forget

"Sing praises to the Lord, enthroned in Zion; proclaim among the nations what He has done." (Psalm 9:11 NIV)

Scripture Focus

"Day after day, in the temple courts and from house to house, they never stopped teaching and proclaiming the good news that Jesus is the Christ." (Acts 5:42, NIV)

"He said to them, 'Go into all the world and preach the good news to all creation.'"(Mark 16:15, NIV)

"For the word of God is living and active." (Hebrews 4:12, NIV)

"For you have been born again, not of perishable seed, but of imperishable, through the living and enduring word of God." (1 Peter 1:23, NIV)

"Jesus answered, 'It is written: "Man does not live on bread alone, but on every word that comes from the mouth of God."'" (Matthew 4:4, NIV)

We Have a Responsibility!

By Dr. Donna Wilcox

Every living, breathing Christian should proactively do something in regards to missions and making sure God's Word is translated into *every* language. Can you imagine the impact we could have in our world if every human being on the planet had access to the Holy Bible!

As you read this chapter, I pray an overwhelming desire will arise within your heart to make a commitment to God (and man) in the pursuit of spreading the Good News in a greater way. The old saying, "Together we can make a difference," still holds true today.

I will begin by giving you a little background about my life. I grew up in a minister's home, and we have an abundance of preachers and evangelists throughout our family. And then there is David Grant. David is one of my first cousins and he not only became an evangelist, but he chose the life of a missionary.

God called David to a land that was very mysterious to most people, especially in the late 1960s and early 1970s. He called him to Calcutta, India. Some of my fondest childhood memories consist of visits David made to our church when he came back to the States to itinerate for his missionary work. He was a dynamo when he preached and never stood still. It was exciting! He shared stories about his many adventures in Calcutta and how God used him (and others) to spread the hope of Jesus to the lost and hurting.

During one of David's visits to our church, my girlfriend and I knelt down in front of the pew where we were sitting and gave our hearts to the Lord; I was eight years old at the time. I always loved the Lord and felt his presence in my young life, but it was the first time I actually asked Jesus Christ to forgive my sins, come into my heart, and become Lord of my life. When I reflect back on that moment, I still remember the overwhelming feeling of love I experienced when I prayed that day. Due to serious health issues, God's unconditional love sustained me during the hard years that followed and continues to do so today.

If you read my autobiography, *Falling into Faith,* you know that I suffered many things due to sickness. It started during childhood and continued throughout my teenage and young-adult years. I remember praying the following prayer at a very young age and throughout my life; "Dear God, before I die I want to make sure others know that Jesus loves them. Help me make a difference!"

I never knew what it meant to be shy, and sharing the love of Christ always stayed on my heart. In fact, it became a motivating reason to live. God performed the miraculous in my life on numerous occasions but I can honestly say I never dreamed one day I would have the opportunity to share Jesus and testify of His miracle-working power outside the United States; much less beyond the Southern States. But we serve a great big, wonderful God!

I remember thinking how brave my cousin David must be. My ever present health issues allowed me to only daydream of doing the things he accomplished for Christ in such an impoverished faraway land. At that time in my young life, the small amount of faith I clung to was weak and battered. Every day presented a new obstacle and challenge to overcome, but God knew a secret. He knew one day I would learn how to grow my faith and dare to believe for the impossible. Once again, we serve a great big, wonderful God!

This gives you a little background into where I came from, and how missions became an important part of my life. To know my story in its entirety, I want to encourage you to read my autobiography, *Falling into Faith*. God performed a miracle of healing in my body, mind, and spirit; of which I am forever grateful. To Him be all the praise and glory!

Now sit back and let the Holy Spirit speak to your heart as I take you back to when Bob and I served as missionaries. During those years we spent some of our time stateside, several years back and forth to Mexico, and eventually God led us to India. Being in these countries opened our eyes to the poverty and pain of so many beautiful people scattered about; trying to survive in barrios, on the streets, as well as in slums and villages.

It is difficult to comprehend the extravagance and how spoiled we are in America until you spend time working and living among the poor and hurting from other nations. I believe everyone who is physically able needs to experience at least one mission's trip in their life. And every Believer should offer some kind of support to those currently on the mission field!

There are times my heart literally aches for the precious people the Lord brought into our lives from the countries we served in. We long for the day we can once again laugh and pray with them face to face. Until that time we will continue to intercede on their behalf, lift a prayer covering over their lives, and help send others out to the field until we can join them once again.

Our days in India were incredibly rewarding. Yes, the overwhelming poverty and despair we saw on a daily basis proved hard, but then life is hard regardless of geography. We walked to work every day alongside all kinds of animals; cows, pigs, donkeys, camels, and the list goes on and on. But sometimes we rode to our destination in a rickshaw.

Riding in a rickshaw was one of my favorite things to do; however, being a blonde and fair-skinned woman in India made it humorous and challenging. The drivers seemed to have a difficult time figuring out where I wanted to go. MG Road is where all the popular shops were in the city, and they could not understand why I did not want to go there. Most Indians we encountered believe Americans are rich and spend their days shopping.

Regardless of where I asked the driver to take me, he usually smiled and said, "Ah, MG Road. I take you there!" I would smile back and reply, *"Nay, nay,"* and then proceed to speak the name of the street slowly and clearly (okay, as clear as a Southern woman can talk). When that did not work, I said the name of the street really fast, hoping it might make a difference. No such luck! After a few exasperating attempts, they usually flashed another smile and once again responded with, "Ah, MG Road. I take you there!" It often proved easier to walk a few miles than explain shopping wasn't the desired destination.

Our mission's work in India consisted mainly of discipleship. Bob worked with a precious Christian Indian man who was a mechanical engineer. Due to an export business our host missionaries started as a means to work among the Indians and build relationships, they traveled around the city and worked closely with other businesses. Through this initiative, it not only provided jobs for the locals but opened many doors to share the message of Christ.

I worked at a candle shop our host missionary family started in an effort to reach out to women. It provided jobs for widows, ex-prostitutes, women escaping a life of human trafficking, as well as those with HIV/AIDS. They learned a trade and received a salary. This helped them provide for their families, with a means to get off the streets and find a safe place to live. It also opened doors for discipleship and Bible studies. I spent one-on-one time with each of these precious women on a daily and weekly basis. I counseled them and shared the power Jesus Christ has to heal and restore broken and hurting lives.

Several of the women from the candle shop (and their children) came to live at the House of Hope. The House of Hope offered them a home filled with love and Christ as its foundation. They received discipleship and instructions on safe, sanitary, and practical living applications. We also provided medicines for those suffering with HIV/AIDS. Some of the women that lived there did not work at the candle shop, so I set aside a weekly time to disciple and counsel with them as well.

Sitting and talking with these beautiful women about Jesus became the thing I looked forward to the most. We saw God move in amazing and miraculous ways. Bob and I made a decision to provide each of them with a Bible in their own language. We were fortunate, because it was not difficult to find Bibles in Hindi. This is not the case for many of our missionaries serving in other countries around the world. *We need to do whatever it takes to get God's Word translated into every language!*

One thing I pray the Lord never allows me to forget are the looks on their precious faces, as the women began reading God's Word in their own language for the first time! It did something inside my spirit that is hard to express. It started a fire, a passion so strong and intense. Words just seem too small when I try to describe it. At that moment I realized just how desperately important it is for Believers to join forces and do whatever it takes to get the Bible translated in every language and in the hands of every man, woman, and child. It is *not* enough for us to tell others what God's Word says. They must have the privilege of reading the living, breathing Word of God for themselves! All the discipleship in the world can only do so much. We absolutely must be able to leave His Word in their hands so reading it becomes part of their daily lives.

As missionaries we love to lead people to Christ and disciple them in their walk with God, but then what? What happens when we leave? We may not always be there, and they need to be armed with the sword that will divide God's truth from Satan's lies. As they read and study the Bible, it creates mighty warriors for Christ who will rise up and lead others to salvation. In turn, they become missionaries, teachers, and preachers to their own people. God's Word teaches them something of utmost importance; they have the power in the name of Jesus to lay hands on the sick and by faith believe for healing, as well as cast out demons, and see the miraculous manifested in their lives and the lives of others!

My heart literally aches for missionaries around the world who are begging, praying, and fasting for ways to get the Bible translated in different languages for the people God has called them to minister to. We must all become active participants in this effort. Remember, this is not just any old book. We are giving them the Book of Life; God's living, breathing Word!

The women I discipled came from a Hindu background and this can be a tough belief to penetrate. They will readily accept Jesus, but they usually just add Him to their long list of gods. It takes time and God's Word to disciple them in the truth, which says we should have no other gods for there is only One True God. He alone is to be worshiped and adored!

I pray I never forget their beautiful faces as they read story after story of the power God displayed over idols and gods that were being worshiped throughout the pages of His Word. This had significant meaning to these women because they live in a culture that continues to practice the same beliefs as those from the pages of the Old and New Testament. The following scriptures spoke to their hearts and changed a generational way of thinking for the first time in their lives. *Only a living, breathing God can transform a heart, mind, and life in this way!*

"So, what about eating meat that has been offered to idols? Well, we all know that an idol is not really a god and that there is only one God. There may be so-called gods both in heaven and on earth, and some people actually worship many gods and many lords. But for us, There is one God, the Father, by whom all things were created, and for whom we live. And there is one Lord, Jesus Christ, through whom all things were created, and through whom we live." (1 Corinthians 8:4-6, NLT)

Many of these women were daily beaten and persecuted for turning away from Hinduism and accepting Jesus Christ as their Lord and Savior. Those who went home to the slums and did not live in the House of Hope shared the abuse they endured from the hands of so-called loved ones. When they entered their homes they were required to make a sacrifice to the Hindu gods. If they refused, numerous family members began a beating ritual. Heartbroken, tears streamed down my face as they shared their stories. One of my new precious friends wiped my tears away and said something I shall forever hold dear to my heart. She looked right into my eyes and boldly stated, "Don't cry, Auntie. Thank you for telling me about the One True God! I am happier than I have ever been!"

This kind of courage and strength is undeniably a miracle that only comes from God! Their determination to serve Christ regardless of the cost, combined with the power of the Holy Spirit working in their lives can turn these slums, villages, and eventually their nation toward the One True Living God. They can impact their world in ways we cannot.

Saying goodbye to my newfound family and sisters in Christ proved difficult, but I knew we were leaving them with God's powerful Word. The opportunity to disciple and teach these precious souls gave us the assurance they knew how to search through the Bible and seek truth for themselves. This knowledge brought an unexplainable peace. Oh how my heart longs for every missionary to experience that same peace. The peace that comes from knowing those they are called to minister to will have God's Word in their hands and in their own language!

I hope this story from our days on the mission field ignited a deep desire and determination in your heart to find a way of equipping missionaries with the greatest tool on earth; God's Holy Word. As Believers there is only one choice, and that is to make this a priority in our lives. I also pray it stirs a spirit of prayer and intercession on behalf of those serving in challenging and often dangerous places around the world.

We have the ability to help make an eternal difference in so many lives. This side of Heaven, many of us will never know the results or the amazing ways God will use our giving and times of prayer and intercession. I want to make sure I stay focused and obedient in everything

God is calling me to do on this earth while there is still time. I hope this is your prayer as well!

~The End~

Truth

Allow me to share some information with you about several ministries that are making a huge difference in this world for the glory of God. These organizations are working and producing amazing Kingdom fruit. They are people of great integrity and their focus is obeying God. When you look at the many lives they have touched and forever changed, their ministry needs no defense. As long as I am on this earth I will be a voice for these ministries!

My cousin David has spent the majority of his life as a missionary to India, along with his wife Dr. Beth Grant and their two beautiful daughters, Rebecca and Jennifer. David and Beth are the visionaries and Co-founders of Project Rescue. Project Rescue is a member of the FAAST Alliance (Faith Alliance Against Slavery and Trafficking), in Washington DC, that enables faith-based international organizations to collaborate in fighting sexual slavery and more effectively minister to its victims.

Beth and Cindy Hudlin developed a comprehensive international curriculum called *Hands That Heal,* to train care givers of sex-trafficking victims, published on behalf of FAAST. David and Beth's ministry is strategically focused on the fight to rescue and restore the victims of human trafficking and share the love of Jesus Christ to the lost and hurting. Their mission and message of hope has carried them to over thirty countries around the world.

I am proud of my family and their determination to stay the course and keep their hearts focused toward the things of God. Below is an excerpt from their website; www.projectrescue.com.

"For 35 years, India has been the heart and focus of David's ministry. Thousands of churches have been planted, and scores of colleges established as a result of his boundless energy. While continuing his commitment to the needs of India, David is increasingly engaged in casting vision and the development of new Homes of Hope across the former Soviet nations.

"Beth's personal calling and passion is that of a teacher. She has served as faculty and guest lecturer in cross-cultural education and women's issues in colleges in India, Europe, and the United States. She also ministers as a guest speaker at women's retreats in Europe, Southern Asia, and America, inspiring women to fulfill God's purposes for their lives and to courageously touch their world with the transforming love and power of Jesus Christ.

"David and Beth have two daughters, Rebecca, age 25, and Jennifer, age 21, who share their parents' heart for ministry to victims of forced prostitution. Rebecca graduated from Evangel University and recently completed a master's program at Missouri State University in theater arts. Jennifer is currently a senior nursing student at Evangel University."

When David first arrived in Calcutta he stayed with Huldah and Mark Buntain. They served as mentors to him and so many others. The Buntains are known around the world for the things they have accomplished in India through the leading and power of the Holy Spirit. They have built more than 700 churches, an educational system with 100-plus schools, and over 30,000 students. Their hospital serves over 100,000 patients yearly. They have a feeding program that feeds over 25,000 people daily, not to mention a school of nursing and a program for the blind. This ministry is still going strong with new projects in the works. God truly is a great big, wonderful God!

Mark Buntain went to be with the Lord in 1989, and God led Huldah to stay in India and continue their work. Their daughter, Bonnie Buntain Long, is a Critical Care nurse and serves as the president of Calcutta Mercy Ministries. Bonnie's husband Jim is a cardio-thoracic surgeon and serves as president of the Calcutta Mercy Hospital. This family has ministered in India for over 50 years. Their mercy ministries are amazing and continue to raise up Christians in India who become preachers, teachers, doctors, nurses, and more! For more information about the Buntain's, please visit their website; www.buntain.org.

If you do not currently support a missionary, please check out these ministries and see what God is doing. If you choose to become a partner, God will bless you and your giving will go toward things that have eternal value.

Don't just give of your finances, also pray! Intercede on behalf of our pastors, evangelists, and missionaries at home and abroad. Intercede for those who are using their gifts all over the world to offer hope and a better life for the broken and hurting. Prayer is powerful, but we must purpose in our hearts to set aside time each day to tap into that power and not only talk, *but listen.* The Creator of all things is our Father, and He still speaks to His people today!

If you attend a church that is not focused on missions, talk to your pastor. Share the desire in your heart to help those spreading the hope of Christ to a lost and dying world. Start a prayer party in your church. That's right—prayer can be a party, and a fun one at that!

There are times when we may feel the need to agonize and wail before God, but prayer does not have to be that way all the time. God is our Father; just make time to talk to Him. We can do it privately as well as in a group. He loves sweet fellowship with His children.

During prayer times be specific, especially when you are aware of certain needs or issues. Remember, the most important ingredient in prayer is faith. *Always pray in faith.* If you are interceding on behalf of others (whether they are missionaries or your neighbor down the street), pray for the things you know about first. Then ask the Holy Spirit to intercede on their behalf in every area of their lives. The Holy Spirit knows how to get right to the heart of the matter!

"In the same way, the Spirit helps us in our weakness. We do not know what we ought to pray for, but the Spirit himself intercedes for us with groans that words cannot express. And he who searches our hearts knows the mind of the Spirit, because the Spirit intercedes for the saints in accordance with God's will." (Romans 8:26-27, NIV)

I want to leave you with one more challenge. Allow me to *strongly* encourage each of you who purchased this book to become part of an organization involved in translating the Bible into other languages. After researching numerous organizations, I have listed some websites below to check out. If you have questions, e-mail or call the organizations. You can also contact me through my website, http://www.donnawilcox.com.

Our church sponsors the "Fire Bible." It is an excellent program centered on spreading the message of Christ through translating the Bible in other languages. All of these organizations need our help, and they are filled with amazing people who have a passion for the lost.

By sowing into these projects you will become a vital part of getting the Word of God to unreached places in this world and into a language others can read and understand. I strongly encourage you to prayerfully consider supporting one or more of these organizations.

http://www.ibs.org
http://www.biblesfortheworld.org
http://www.gideons.org
http://ag.org

I pray you will accept this challenge and become a partner in the mission of getting God's Word translated into every tongue and in the hands of every tribe and nation. I also pray a missionary is added to your monthly support and prayer list. Tell your friends and ask them to do the same!

Christians have a responsibility. People are hurting, and many have not heard of our wonderful Savior. They need to know there is God who loves them and longs to be their Healer, Redeemer, Father, and Friend! He is not some obscure and distant character. We are all made in His image and likeness; therefore, the Lord feels, He sees, and He longs for a growing, nurturing, and personal relationship with every one of us.

As long as our motives are pure and line up with God's Word, then we can pray in faith and know that the Father is faithful to hear and answer our prayers.

"Ask and it shall be given to you; seek and you will find; knock and the door will be opened to you. For everyone who asks receives; he who seeks finds; and to him who knocks, the door will be opened." (Matthew 7:7-8, NIV)

"You do not have because you do not ask God. When you ask, you do not receive, because you ask with wrong motives, that you may spend what you get on your pleasures." (James 4:2-3, NIV)

It is time to look beyond our own comfortable and safe surroundings and do something that can change the lives of others for eternity. For those of you who will raise the banner high and join this mission; *thank you and God bless you!*

If you are reading this chapter and have practiced a lifestyle of giving along with prayer and intercession, you are my heroes! Thank you for the example of Christ you have been and continue to be. *I pray that you experience an overwhelming increase in every area of your lives!*

"Then the King will say to those on his right, 'Come, you who are blessed by my Father, inherit the Kingdom prepared for you from the creation of the world. For I was hungry, and you fed me. I was thirsty, and you gave me a drink. I was a stranger, and you invited me into your home. I was naked, and you gave me clothing. I was sick, and you cared for me. I was in prison, and you visited me.'

"Then these righteous ones will reply, 'Lord, when did we ever see you hungry and feed you? Or thirsty and give you something to drink? Or a stranger and show you hospitality? Or naked and give you clothing? When did we ever see you sick or in prison and visit you?'

"And the King will say, 'I tell you the truth, when you did it to one of the least of these my brothers and sisters, you were doing it to me!' (Matthew 25: 34-40, NIV, emphasis added)

Chapter 11

A Lesson in Refining

"Yet, O Lord, You are our Father. We are the clay, you are the Potter; we are all the work of Your hand." (Isaiah 64:8, NIV)

Scripture Focus

"But who are you, O man, to talk back to God? Shall what is formed say to him who formed it, "Why did you make me like this?" Does not the Potter have the right to make out of the same lump of clay some pottery for noble purposes and some for common use?" (Romans 9:20-21, NIV)

"This is the word that came to Jeremiah from the Lord: 'Go down to the potter's house, and there I will give you My message.' So I went down to the potter's house, and I saw him working at the wheel. But the pot he was shaping from the clay was marred in his hands; so the potter formed it into another pot, shaping it as seemed best to him. Then the word of the Lord came to me: *'O house of Israel, can I not do with you as this potter does?'* declares the Lord. *'Like clay in the hand of the potter, so are you in My hand,* O house of Israel.'" (Jeremiah 18:1-6, NIV, emphasis added)

Our Refiner and Purifier

By Dr. Donna Wilcox

"He will sit as a refiner and purifier of silver." (Malachi 3:3, NIV). This verse is a beautiful illustration of the Potter and the clay, and the deep commitment God has toward His children! It truly makes a magnificent

116

statement about the character and nature of God. To understand why, we must take a look at the process of refining silver. Once we do this we can catch a glimpse into the patience, love, and skill our Heavenly Father puts into molding our lives into something of worth.

Silversmiths work with and form silver, for example; to make jewelry. To do their job they use many tools, such as: a smoldering torch, piercing saw, files, mallets, hammers, pickling acid, and a polishing machine. Silversmiths grasp a piece of silver with a tool as they hold it over fire to let it heat up. They are particularly careful to hold the silver in the middle of the fire where the flames are the hottest, making sure to burn away all the impurities.

Think about this for a moment and reflect on the scripture, "He sits as a refiner and purifier of silver." When life is hard and we feel like we are being held over the fire, never forget God is there and He is holding us in the palm of His hand. If we are patient and allow Him to work in our lives, the impurities which prevent us from experiencing victory will be destroyed!

There is one more thing we need to understand about a silversmith. He carefully keeps his eye on the silver and sits in front of the fire holding the silver the entire time it is being refined. He knows something important; if the silver is left a moment too long in the flames, it will be destroyed.

When we give God permission to work in our lives we will not be destroyed! The result is something amazing. We become vessels of beauty which can be used for His glory in powerful ways.

~ The End ~

Truth

Our Creator, God the Father, is *All-Powerful* and *Sovereign.* His purposes for His creations will be fulfilled. Like the potter who creates each pot, bowl, or cup to meet a specific objective, God forms each one of us with His plans for our lives in mind.

Just as a potter kneads clay to remove impurities and air bubbles, God removes impurities to make us useful and fruitful for His service. Just as a potter turns the wheel and shapes the clay into a useful vessel, so God uses the turning of events to shape His children; His precious ones! When we are being held in that "hot spot" He never leaves us alone. He knows the outcome will bring forth beauty and an intimacy with Him.

Because of the New Covenant God has established with us through Jesus Christ, we can trust the Master Potter to work out our imperfections and gently mold us into the likeness of His Son.

"We are assured and know that [God being a partner in their labor] all things work together and are [fitting into a plan] for good to and for those who love God and are called according to [His] design and purpose." (Romans 8:28, AMP)

We have a choice in how we respond to the reality of this truth. We can rebel against God and resent Him because we don't like what we see or feel, or we can take comfort in the fact He is carefully molding us into something beautiful. He is meticulously working out every detail to ensure success and victory as we meet and overcome each challenge life brings. If we learn to hang on and trust God, we will bring glory to His name and *lack no good thing.*

"For the LORD God is a sun and shield; The LORD gives grace and glory; No good thing does He withhold from those who walk uprightly." (Psalm 84:11, NASB)

"For the LORD God is our sun and our shield. He gives us grace and glory. The LORD will withhold no good thing from those who do what is right." (Psalm 34:10, NLT)

You are never so messed up, so marred, that Father God cannot create something miraculous and glorious out of your life! He longs to safely hold you, lovingly mold you, as He forms a trusting and intimate relationship with you this very day. How will you respond?

Chapter 12

Peace of Mind

"You will keep in perfect peace him whose mind is steadfast, because he trusts in You. Trust in the Lord forever, for the Lord, the Lord, is the Rock eternal." (Isaiah 26:3-4, NIV)

Scripture Focus

"The Lord gives strength to His people; the Lord blesses His people with peace." (Psalm 29:11, NIV)

"Because of the tender mercy of our God, by which the rising sun will come to us from heaven to shine on those living in darkness and in the shadow of death, to guide our feet into the path of peace." (Luke 1:79, NIV)

"Now may the Lord of peace Himself give you peace at all times and in every way. The Lord be with all of you." (2 Thessalonians 3:16, NIV)

Peace in the Midst of a Trial

By Linda Chessher

In loving memory of my sister Ouida, who went to be with the Lord March 17, 2008

My husband Nathan went in the hospital on April 21, 2006, with acute pneumonia. X-rays showed one lung collapsed, and the other one was a third of the way full of fluid. They called in a surgeon, and he ordered additional x-rays. The report came back showing his left lung had an infection so severe it had exploded through the wall of the lung. The lung created pockets around the bottom of it to hold the infection, causing the lung to die and a crustation to form behind it. The doctors said antibiotics would not touch the infection, and they needed to do surgery to remove about a third of the lung and the crustation.

Surgery was scheduled for the following Monday, but the Friday before they did a CT scan. On Saturday, they came back with some disturbing news. They said the surgery had to be put on hold because the CT scan showed a mass tumor over the top of Nathan's lung. They did a needle biopsy, but it failed, so the doctor scheduled an incision biopsy. When the surgery was over he came out to inform us he had to remove a lot more than he anticipated. He then stated, "It looks bad, and I feel certain Nathan has lymphoma cancer." We were shaken, but in the midst of it all we started a prayer chain for Nathan. I called Donna, Bob, my Pastor, and many others to pray and intercede on our behalf.

On May 21 we were scheduled to see an oncologist. He had not received the results of Nathan's test because they were having a difficult time diagnosing the cancer. He suggested we go ahead and schedule for a port to be put in so that we would not lose any time getting him started on chemotherapy treatment. We declined, stating we wanted to wait for the results.

Finally the results arrived with some unwanted news. Nathan was diagnosed with thymoma cancer, which is very rare. They also told us he needed to see a surgeon in Pensacola, Florida. I prayed for direction and wisdom, because the doctors did not seem to know a lot about thymoma. With the help of my sister Ouida, I found H. Lee Moffitt Cancer Center in Tampa, Florida. I called them, and they accepted his case, scheduling surgery for July 13, 2006.

We arrived at the cancer center with all of Nathan's CT scan's and test results. We talked to the doctor assigned to Nathan's case, and he stated, "Well it looks as if the lung surgery needs to be taken care of as well as the cancer surgery." We asked him if he could do both surgeries at the same time, but he was not sure. Then he said, "Let me have another scan made before I let you go." This is when things turned interesting and miraculous! He came back stating, "Well, it looks as if the lung has cleared up except for a small amount of fluid in it, and the lung surgery will *not* be necessary." Praise God! This was miracle number one.

On July 13, 2006, the doctor took out Nathan's thymus gland and the tumor. He said the tumor was encapsulated and had not spread. Miracle number two! Nathan was released from the hospital on Sunday. They sent the tumor to be tested and advised us that further treatment would depend on the stage and progression of the cancer. We went back two weeks later for the results, and they said no other treatment would be necessary: Miracle number three. Praise God!

In the beginning of this trial when our world was falling apart, I thought about all the times I heard Christians say how God gave them a special scripture during a trial or hardship. That day, as I sat down to do my devotion I opened the Bible and saw this scripture: "Thou wilt keep him in perfect peace, whose mind is stayed on Thee: because he trusteth in Thee. Trust ye in the LORD forever: for in the LORD JEHOVAH is everlasting strength." (Isaiah 26:3, 4, KJV)

During those dark days of waiting and not knowing, I held on tight to these two verses. God is Awesome, Faithful, and True. Prayer truly changed things and gave us miracle after miracle. We are so thankful for Bob, Donna, and so many others who prayed and encouraged us along the way.

~The End~

Truth

Linda is a precious friend God gave me when I worked at a call center in Florida. We worked in a stressful environment, and our friendship made coming to work more enjoyable. The Lord blessed us with an immediate kinship and sisterhood. Together we joined with other Christians and prayed for each other's needs, as well as requests brought to us throughout the office. Time after time, we witnessed the miracle hand of God as He answered prayer and moved mightily in our lives and those around us.

When Bob and I met Linda's husband Nathan, our families formed a lasting bond of love and friendship. They became faithful supporters of our mission's work and we are so thankful for how they blessed our lives and the lives of so many others.

Linda and Nathan are active in the Muscogee Nation of Florida, (a.k.a. Florida tribe of the Eastern Creek Indians), and with God's help they bring a Biblical and Christian influence into this culture. His power demonstrated through their lives and testimonies continues to bring the realization to many in this tribe that God is The One and Only True God.

When we heard of Nathan's illness we immediately hit our knees in prayer. God is the Great Physician, and *through Him, all things are possible.* Holding on to that truth we all began praying healing scriptures over Nathan, making the scriptures personal by putting his name in each one. Prayers were going up everywhere on behalf of both of them. Intercessory prayer touches the heart of God in a powerful way, and He heard our cries and healed Nathan's body. God is good!

What I love about this testimony is how God answered Linda's prayer through His Word, and how she held on *in faith* to His promise of peace. Did they ever get scared? Yes! However, they did not let go of God's hand, and they stood firm in the fact He is a loving and faithful Father.

I recorded twelve songs which can be downloaded from my website free of charge. One of those songs in particular came to mind as I read Linda and Nathan's story. It says, "In the midst of it all, I shall stand and not fall, and bless His name." There is power in praising God and standing strong, even when things look bad and our faith feels weak and inadequate.

Our praise should not be based on conditions or circumstances. We should praise Him at all times, not just when things are good and life is great. The power of praise opens the door for miracles to manifest in our lives. Try this praise principle today and hold on to God's Word, just like Nathan and Linda chose to do.

Bob and I are blessed with amazing friends who continue to live their lives for the cause of Christ, and share the truth of His resurrecting power. Through their testimonies, I pray you catch a glimpse of His overwhelming love and the fact *He truly is the God of the Impossible!*

"Be joyful always; pray continually; *give thanks in all circumstances*, for this is God's will for you in Christ Jesus." (1 Thessalonians 5:16-18, NIV, emphasis added)

"But thanks be to God! He gives us the victory through our Lord Jesus Christ. Therefore, my dear brother, stand firm. Let nothing move you. Always give yourselves fully to the work of the Lord, because you know that your labor in the Lord is not in vain." (1 Corinthians 15:57-58, NIV)

"You turned my wailing into dancing; You removed my sackcloth and clothed me with joy, that my heart may sing to You and not be silent. O Lord my God, I will give You thanks forever." (Psalm 30:11-12, NIV)

Chapter 13

Messin' with the Devil

"They overcame him by the blood of the Lamb and the word of their testimony; they did not love their lives so much as to shrink from death." (Revelation 12:11, NIV)

Scripture Focus

"Consider it pure joy, my brothers, whenever you face trials of many kinds, because you know that the testing of your faith develops perseverance. Perseverance must finish its work so that you may be mature and complete, *not lacking anything!*" (James 1:2-4, NIV, emphasis added)

"My son, attend to My words; incline thine ear unto My sayings. Let them not depart from thine eyes; keep them in the midst of thine heart. For they are life unto those that find them, and health to all their flesh." (Proverbs 4:20-22, KJV)

Going on the Offense

By Dr. Donna Wilcox

Throughout my life I suffered with bladder and kidney infections, but God consistently came through in amazing ways. Two weeks prior to leaving for missionary school, I came down with a painful bladder infection which seemed to be advancing into my kidneys. I did not want to go to the doctor, but I knew if the symptoms persisted it was inevitable.

The timing of this illness along with how suddenly it hit me, felt like an attack. Bob and I realized the enemy wanted us to think twice about our decision to become missionaries. With all the serious health issues I had encountered, pursuing this journey seemed incredulous!

It is important to understand something about faith and the unknown; when God calls you to step out in faith and embark on a new journey, He will equip you with the wisdom and strength to accomplish *all* He has called you to do. The road may be hard, but *His grace is sufficient* and *His strength is more than enough!*

As you read the following story taken from my autobiography, you will understand why this experience forever changed the way I approach trials and adversity.

Excerpt from *Falling into Faith,* Chapter 23, *Missionary School... Here We Come!*

"Going into missions means going to places where hospitals are rare and doctors are not always reliable. The right medications can be hard to come by, and it really is a step of faith for someone who has had numerous health issues. As Bob and I prepared to leave the security of home to go into the unknown, Satan desperately tried to get as many punches in as possible in an effort to get our eyes focused on the 'good and comfortable life,' wanting us to shrink back and change our minds. His plans failed miserably; instead, it created more of a determination in our hearts to walk the path of obedience and trust God.

"Perplexed over this bladder infection and struggling with pain, Bob looked at me and said, 'Baby, maybe we should try something different and go on the offense. Tell the Devil to bring on the symptoms. As he tries to afflict you, purpose to go out and talk to anyone you meet about Jesus. Tell them all the healings and miracles God has given you. We will get him where it hurts!' Then Bob reminded me of Revelation 12:11, 'They overcame him by the blood of the Lamb and the word of their testimony; they did not love their lives so much as to shrink from death.'

"I cannot explain it, but my spirit jumped and caused me to go into immediate action when he spoke those words. Fearing the mission field or anything else because of past health issues was no longer an option. At

that moment, I realized if I died while telling others about Jesus, at least I would be giving something in return for all He had done for me. God brought me this far; He would victoriously take me all the way!

"With that in mind, I got on the phone and called three very dear friends (Linda, Elaine, and Maxine). I knew they would do anything in the world for me. I asked them if illness ever interfered with my ability to minister, would they hit the streets on my behalf and tell others how Jesus miraculously healed me of cancer (and any other testimony they wanted to share) until I was able to continue the work God called me to do. Without hesitation, they all said, YES! After hanging up the phone, I expressed loudly and with authority in Jesus name, 'Devil, the battle lines are drawn.' I advised the enemy to go ahead and bring it on. Not only would I boldly testify for Jesus with every pain and symptom, but my friends were also prepared to go for me. ... Numbers are powerful in the spirit realm!

"We went to bed that night full of determination, but I awoke the next morning feeling worse, making me even madder. I dressed, kissed my husband, and headed out the door exclaiming, 'I'm off to witness for Jesus. The Devil must have thought we were kidding.' Bob gave me a big hug as I got in the car and drove away. I immediately felt impressed to go to the hospital and knew it must be God, because it is one of my least favorite things to do in the entire world.

"Making a quick detour, I went by a Christian Book Store and bought crosses with the sinner's prayer printed on them and scripture cards filled with God's promises and blessings. Within minutes, I sat in the hospital parking lot telling the Devil just how sorry he would be before the day was over!

"I entered the hospital armed with goodies and the joy of the Lord. A nurse stopped and asked if she could help me. (I must have looked lost.) I told her I had some gifts to hand out to anyone who needed someone to talk with or wanted prayer. She ushered me down the hall to a room and said, 'You can start here. Everyone on this floor could use some encouragement.'

"The Holy Spirit prepared the way as I entered each room. The patients were kind and receptive, expressing appreciation for the gifts I *left with them. Although most of them did not know Jesus as their Savior, they welcomed prayer and listened as I shared my healing testimony.*

"Something wonderful happened as I went from room to room praying and testifying about the goodness of the Lord. The pain, burning, and pressure in my bladder and lower back gradually subsided. By the time I finished praying for everyone on that floor the pain had disappeared.

"I stepped outside the hospital doors completely healed and feeling victoriously refreshed. As I walked toward the car and passed the emergency room entrance, something inside my spirit said, 'You aren't through yet!' I was having so much fun messing with the Devil and getting points in for the 'good guys' that I stopped, backed up, and went in.

"A young couple was sitting by the nurse's station, and they were quite a remarkable sight. Both of their bodies were tattooed all over with pierced eyebrows, lips, nose, and Lord only knows what else! A normal person might have felt a little afraid or intimidated to strike up a conversation and boldly ask, 'May I pray for you?' Not me; by this time I felt like I could take on an army.

"I sat down next to them and proceeded to testify about how God healed me of cancer, explaining His power to redeem and restore lives. Before I could even finish and with tears in his eyes, this precious young man asked me to pray for his brother. He said something was wrong, and the doctors had not been able to figure out the problem. I immediately took their hands and began praying. As I got up to leave, I gave them a cross and scripture card and asked them to read the Bible and keep talking to God. I assured them of His ability to hear and answer prayer. They nodded, thanked me, and shook my hand.

"Looking around, I realized the only other people in the emergency room were a little girl and her mother. The child loudly asked, 'Mom, can she pray for me?' Walking over, I told the young woman I would be happy to pray for her daughter. She seemed a bit reluctant, but the little girl persisted. (I love children!)

"I briefly went over my healing testimony again (knowing they overheard most of it already) and asked how I could pray. They were vacationing in Destin at the beach when the little girl came out of the water with red swollen welts all over her body. I could see red puffy marks on her arms and legs, so I took them by the hands and prayed

a simple prayer of faith. I gave them my last cross and scripture card, encouraging them to read their Bibles and discover all the wonderful things about God and His power to heal and bless all who believe in Him. I sensed this little girl had faith and believed what I said. Before leaving, she reached up and gave me a great big hug.... God is so good!

"I sat in the parking lot crying tears of joy as I called Bob on the cell phone and shared what God accomplished in those few hours. He was ecstatic! It boosted our faith in such a real and tangible way. We grew even more excited about what the future held, knowing the Father would take good care of us."

~The End~

Truth

The Bible is full of stories about the Lord's amazing ability to crush and destroy the enemy. When you actually experience a victory like this, it strengthens your faith and offers a glimpse into the power God can manifest in our lives when we *exercise our faith, rise up,* and *choose to believe!*

I am truly changed by this experience and when I reflect back on what happened that day, I feel a charge of excitement go through my entire body. It reminds me of God's ability to carry us through to victory in unusual and wonderful ways when we become an active participant with Him.

One important way to participate and live a victorious and overcoming life is to share your testimony. The Bible says, "And they defeated him by the blood of the Lamb, and by the word of their testimony. And they did not love their lives so much that they were afraid to die." (Revelation 12:11, NLT). The blood of the Lamb was shed on the cross at Calvary. Jesus Christ fulfilled His part; now it is up to us to do ours. *Testify!*

Let's take a moment to study the following scriptures in James. I will use the Amplified Version to bring clarity and offer a deeper insight into the wisdom God's Word teaches us about trials and temptations. When we actually apply these principles to our lives, we will become mature in our

Christian walk and begin understanding what it means to overcome. Our testimony grows powerful in word and deed, and the lost will actually want what we have and pursue God!

"Consider it wholly joyful, my brethren, whenever you are enveloped in *or* encounter trials of any sort *or* fall in various temptations. Be assured *and* understand that the trial *and* proving of your faith bring out endurance *and* steadfastness *and* patience. But let endurance *and* steadfastness *and* patience have full play *and* do a thorough work, so that you may be (people) perfectly and fully developed (with no defects), lacking in nothing. If any of you is deficient in wisdom, let him ask of "the giving God" (who gives) to everyone liberally *and* ungrudgingly, without reproaching *or* faultfinding, and it will be given him." (James 1:2-5, AMP)

As wonderful as these scriptures are, let's read the next few verses. It is the key to what our mindset must be in order for God to answer our prayers!

"Only it must be in faith that he asks with no wavering (no hesitating, no doubting). For the one who wavers (hesitates, doubts) is like the billowing surge out at sea that is blown hither *and* thither and tossed by the wind. *For truly, let not such a person imagine that he will receive anything (he asks for) from the Lord.* (For being as he is) a man of two minds (hesitating, dubious, irresolute), (he is) unstable and unreliable and uncertain about everything (he thinks, feels, decides)." (James 1:6-8, AMP, emphasis added)

These verses are powerful! Being obedient to God's Word does not mean you won't have doubts and fears. Should we be ashamed and feel condemnation when we do? No! However, a person who is truly trusting God will take Him at His Word, dare to keep believing, and constantly feed their faith—*in spite of those doubts!* This is the kind of love walk that sees results and produces lasting Kingdom fruit for the glory of God.

I want my life to be a testimony of God's power. Don't you? Ask God to strengthen your heart and mind and apply His Word to whatever you are facing. With unwavering determination, relentlessly pursue God. Your *faith in action* will pave the way for the miraculous to burst forth in your life! Below are a few amazing examples of *faith in action!*

Jesus Heals in Response to Faith (Matthew 9:18-26, NLT)

"As Jesus was saying this, the leader of a synagogue came and knelt before him. "My daughter has just died," he said, "but you can bring her back to life again if you just come and lay your hand on her." So Jesus and his disciples got up and went with him."

"Just then a woman who had suffered for twelve years with constant bleeding came up behind him. She touched the fringe of his robe, for she thought, "If I can just touch his robe, I will be healed." "Jesus turned around, and when he saw her he said, *"Daughter, be encouraged! Your faith has made you well."* And the woman was healed at that moment."

"When Jesus arrived at the official's home, he saw the noisy crowd and heard the funeral music. "Get out!" he told them. "The girl isn't dead; she's only asleep." But the crowd laughed at him. After the crowd was put outside, however, Jesus went in and took the girl by the hand, and she stood up! The report of this miracle swept through the entire countryside."

Jesus Heals the Blind (Matthew 9:27-29, NLT)

"After Jesus left the girl's home, two blind men followed along behind him, shouting, "Son of David, have mercy on us!" They went right into the house where he was staying, and Jesus asked them, *"Do you believe I can make you see?"* "Yes, Lord," they told him, "we do." Then he touched their eyes and said, *"Because of your faith, it will happen."*

Chapter 14

Against the Odds

"And Jesus said, 'Suffer little children, and forbid them not, to come unto me; for of such is the kingdom of heaven.'" (Matthew 19:14, KJV)

Scripture Focus

"Then the King will say to those on his right, 'Come, you who are blessed by My Father; take your inheritance, the Kingdom prepared for you since the creation of the world. For I was hungry and you gave me something to eat, I was thirsty and you gave me something to drink, I was a stranger and you invited me in, I needed clothes and you clothed me, I was sick and you looked after me, I was in prison and you came to visit me.' Then the righteous will answer him, 'Lord, when did we see you hungry and feed you, or thirsty and give you something to drink? When did we see you a stranger and invite you in, or needing clothes and clothe you? When did we see you sick or in prison and go to visit you?' The King will reply, 'I tell you the truth, whatever you did for one of the least of these brothers of mine, you did for me.'" (Matthew 25:34-40, NIV)

"Blessed is he whose help is the God of Jacob, whose hope is in the Lord his God, the Maker of heaven and earth, the sea, and everything in them—the Lord, who remains faithful forever. He upholds the cause of the oppressed and gives food to the hungry. The Lord sets prisoners free, the Lord gives sight to the blind, the Lord lifts up those who are bowed down, the Lord loves the righteous. The Lord watches over the alien and sustains the fatherless and the widow, but He frustrates the wicked. The Lord reigns forever, your God, O Zion, for all generations. Praise the Lord." (Psalm 146:5-10, NIV)

We Are a Happy Family!

By Pat Sowell

Labor Day of 2001 appeared to be a typical holiday for my family with the usual barbecue and trimmings. As with many gatherings of this nature, later that evening someone began to have a difference of opinion that escalated into a disturbance. The police was called and because there were minor children present (Tamara and Kayla, twin sisters not yet one, and their two-year-old brother, Mateo), they felt it necessary to remove them from the residence and place them in foster care. Unfortunately, this was not the first incident.

Not wanting the children placed in permanent foster care, where we would be given minimal (or nonexistent) visitation, my family asked if I would be willing to keep the children until the parents got themselves together. I had a good job. I was single with only one child, Erin, a senior in college. I said, "Yes," but without Erin's willingness to assist me with the kids and help financially, I really would not have been able to do this. It seemed quite ironic, though, because I was finally at a place in life where I had begun to experience freedom to travel and just relax, but God saw a different direction for my life.

The children's parents were required to take parenting classes, maintain a household, and prove themselves worthy to raise their children for a continuous six-month period. The children's mother had full-blown sickle cell disease and was unable to care for the children emotionally, physically, and financially. The year I got custody of them she had been hospitalized fifty-six times. Due to both parents' addictions and lifestyles, time would reveal they were not capable to raise these children.

After the State of Florida's screenings and background checks, I received a call on Thursday, September 6, saying everything checked out, and I could have custody the following day at 1 p.m. This just happened to be the twins' first birthday, and we were hoping and praying that they could come home in time to celebrate. God saw fit and made this possible! Tamara, Kayla, and Mateo arrived as promised, and we made arrangements to have a big birthday party and celebration on the following day with cake, ice cream, balloons, and family.

Not being familiar with their mother (other than what I heard from outside sources), I was not sure what role she actually wanted to play in the children's lives. Sometimes you have to just sit back and let whatever is going to happen run its course. The children's well-being continued to be my main concern. God gave me the wisdom to deal with each and every situation, and the little ones were always under His protection.

Since I attended church every Sunday, the kids needed some nicer clothes to wear. Each family member went out and purchased what was needed: Shoes, dresses, pants, socks, and shirts. The next Sunday, I got them ready for church with just enough time to get ready myself. Everything went smoothly. As we all walked in that morning our church family greeted us, while all the curious lookers stared, wondering what in the world was I doing with all these kids. I told the ushers if they saw things begin to get out of hand, such as crying, screaming, and misbehaving, they had my permission to come to my aid and help. The first few months were uneventful, but as the children began to grow and explore, Sunday mornings proved to be a little hectic.

Shortly after getting the children, my job gave me two baby showers to assist with things that I needed for them, and friends and family pitched in when necessary. One thing I received that created a *life-changing* event was a large case of Pampers from Sam's Club, which included a free *Barney and Friends* tape. Thinking they were too young for Barney I just used the diapers and ignored the tape.

As the girls began to toddle around and get into things they were not supposed to, I tried to resolve this by putting them in the baby bed right after their bath until I myself could get dressed. This usually ended up with me having to redo everything because they would undress each other, including taking the barrettes and ribbons out of one another's hair.

One Sunday I put them in the bed and went to take a shower. While I was showering I could hear them laughing. The longer I stayed in the bathroom it seemed the laughing drew closer, and suddenly they were right outside the bathroom door calling me. I panicked and thought someone had gotten into the house and taken them out of the bed. When I looked around I saw their brother. He was still sitting in the same spot where I left him watching television. I questioned him as to how they got out of the bed, and he could not explain it. After carefully looking around, I saw where they had shaken the bed until the bolts had loosened, and they "escaped" out of the bottom! At that moment, I realized just how smart these little ones were, and I knew I had my hands full. After putting the bed back together, I decided to try another approach. I made plans to start getting up before they awoke and quickly shower and get dressed.

Another Sunday rolled around, and we were running late. I needed to take a shower before coming to church and remembered the Barney tape that I had taken out of the Pampers bag and put away. The girls were no longer in diapers, so I thought they might be old enough now to sit and watch it. I put the tape in, turned on the television, and went to take a shower. I hurried, praying they were being good. To my amazement, I did not hear one word the whole time I was in the shower. When I stepped out of the bathroom I nervously expected the worst, but believe it or not, they were in the exact same spot where I had left them, still watching Barney! From that day forward I have always considered Barney as one of my favorite friends.

I acquired every Barney tape that I could get my hands on, and when I had something I needed to do without being disturbed (like cooking, washing, or showering), I just popped one in and turned on the television. It worked every time! One day I came into the room, and the three of them were lying in the floor singing the Barney song and when they reached the part that said, "We are a happy family," I knew the decision I made to keep this family together was a good one.

During a particularly stressful day at work, I received several phone calls from the day care about the girls and the preschool about Mateo. It began to dawn on me just how desperately I needed some help, especially with Mateo. I decided to ask Donna if she and Bob could relieve me by taking him on some weekends. I felt he could use a father figure, and I trusted Bob and Donna to be a Christian example. I also knew they would shower him with a lot of love and attention. I could see having twin baby sisters to contend with was not always easy for the little fellow. They happily agreed, and I felt blessed to have someone I could trust helping me with him. Mateo loved going to "Mr. Bob's and Ms. Donna's!"

Throughout these times of adjustments, there were difficult obstacles to overcome, as well as days when I lost my patience. In those moments, the Lord reminded me of all the displacement and other things these children had suffered during the time they were with their mother. That reality brought a sense of peace and comfort to the decision I made to take them into my home and raise them as my own.

My friend Donna gave me a tape of twelve songs she recorded in a studio for her father before leaving for missions. One night as I listened to those songs I awoke to what I thought was a dream. I could plainly see Donna singing, "His Grace Still Amazes Me," and it seemed as if she sang it directly to me. I felt as if every word in that song held a personal message from the Lord meant just for me!

I have truly been amazed at God's grace throughout this situation. With a grateful heart, I am thankful for friends like Donna and Bob, Elaine, Tonya, Jean, and so many others, who daily interceded and prayed for us. We could not have endured some of the things we walked through without their love, prayers, and support. I always say, "God puts people in our lives for a reason. They may not be there a lifetime, but they are there when it is necessary for us to go through the rough times as well as the good ones." I have also witnessed the truth and peace of God's promise to "never leave or forsake us."

The kids and I, (as well as all of my family and friends) are a happy family. Between Youth Choir and Monday Night Youth Outreach, we have become more and more active in church. Through these functions, they received help with homework along with some much-needed encouragement and spiritual guidance. We are blessed, and I pray each day that God continues to give me the wisdom to make us a "Happy Family."

~The End~

Truth

Pat is another dear friend God gave me when I worked at a call center in Florida. She had been with the telephone company for over twenty years, and just like many others, found it hard to adjust to a huge corporation coming in and making so many changes. Their small family had been pulled apart and new faces were everywhere.

Pat is a very private and reserved person, but we soon became great friends. As sisters in the Lord, we prayed for one another and enjoyed sharing our faith and love for Christ. She rarely discussed her personal life, so I felt honored when she told me about taking these children in as her own to love and raise. I knew this had to be a God thing, and huge blessings would come from her selfless and loving act of kindness.

Pat did not know it, but for some time Bob and I had been praying for God to send a young person in our lives to mentor and love. From the time we got married our home had been a safe haven for young people, but suddenly we found ourselves alone with no one to nurture and sow into. Not even a week before Pat asked for our help, Bob specifically said to me, "I think I would enjoy helping a younger child who needs a father figure, not necessarily a teenager." I happily agreed but wondered out loud, "Who? And where do we find someone?" Our home always bustled about with teens or young adults so we decided to pray for God to send a child, and He used Pat to lovingly answer our prayers!

The call center changed things around (again), and Pat and I ended up being put on the same team and sitting next to one another. One day she looked at me and said, "Donna, I have a question to ask you, but I don't want you to give me answer right away. Go home and talk to Bob and pray about it first."

I replied, "Okay, what is it?"

She proceeded to ask if Bob and I would take Mateo every other weekend and spend time with him.

Before she could even finish I excitedly answered, "Yes...Yes... YES!" She immediately said to talk to Bob first, but I interrupted and excitedly stated, "I am going to call Bob right now. This is exactly what we asked God to do for us." I then told her how we had been praying for God to send a young child our way that we could love and mentor. She looked stunned, but very happy and relieved. Pat isn't one to ask for help, and I knew this was difficult for her.

I ran into my manager's office and called Bob on the phone. I talked so fast I don't know if he fully understood what I was saying. Thankfully, he has lived with me long enough and learned how to interpret my crazy, sporadic ramblings! Bob immediately praised God for answered prayer and wanted to know if Mateo could come the upcoming weekend.

Putting him on hold I ran and asked Pat for permission and she said, "Yes!"

This precious little boy possessed such a loving and sweet nature considering all he had experienced in his young life. I think he sensed my need to *mama him* and always gave me a lot of affection. His beautiful smile lit up a room and he constantly focused on pleasing Bob. We sensed he longed for a father's approval. He just beamed when Bob said he did something well or he was proud of him. We even took him on vacation with us to Arkansas to visit our friends Kevin and Kara. Mateo kept everyone entertained, and he enjoyed every waking minute of his first big adventure out of Sate!

I cannot begin to tell you the joy Mateo brought into our lives, and although he proved to be a handful at times we are so thankful God sent him to us. The love we received and the things we were able to teach him (not to mention what he taught us), far outweighed all the obstacles and challenges we faced.

As we prepared to leave Florida for missionary school in Colorado, the thought of saying goodbye to Mateo felt heart wrenching and painful. Fortunately, Mateo knew how to capture people's hearts, and our neighbors Mike and Liz just fell in love with him. They promised to take him under their wing and help Pat after we left. This truly made the burden so much lighter. In fact, when December of that year rolled around Pat and the kids enjoyed a huge and bountiful Christmas; thanks to Mike, Liz, their church, and many others! When we returned home to Colorado from Mexico in February of 2004, we received a beautiful card from Pat. She shared with us how God blessed them during the holidays. The Lord truly is a faithful Father to the fatherless!

When I think back on our time with Mateo my heart hurts because we miss him. He and his sisters are growing up so fast, and we are not there to see it. Pat sends us pictures and updates about the kids, and it is such a blessing to hear what God continues to do in their lives.

Pat should be awarded sainthood for what she chose to do! She was no longer in her twenties or thirties, yet she lovingly embraced these three needy, hurting, and love-starved children! Even with its pain and trials,

I know for a fact she is thankful for the decision she made to open her heart and home.

Since 1996, Bob and I have been blessed with the privilege of being Mom and Dad to forty-nine young people. Some of them were only for a season, but most of them stuck around and continue to call our house "home." We are beyond blessed! All our kids have heard me repeatedly express on numerous occasions; "My heart is full!"

There was an article written about our rather-large family in Colorado Springs in 2006, and it struck me a little odd at the time. You see, I really did not know we were all that strange. Some have even called us, "Crazy!" I can't blame them. I suppose we are a bit different from your average family. Our gang is made up of all colors, shapes, sizes, and backgrounds. I can tell you this; I agonized for many years over the fact I could never have children of my own, but God's plan to give me a family was so much better than I ever dreamed. Call me crazy (and you may be right), but without hesitation I can proudly proclaim; "Praise God, my heart is full and I am blessed to overflowing!"

You see, during those agonizing and barren years I made a decision. I belong to God, and His Word says I am to be fruitful and multiply. With stubborn determination I held tight to His promises and spent a lot of time on my knees in prayer and fasting. With unwavering faith I believed He would answer the cry of my heart. His plan to bless me with a family topped absolutely anything I ever dared to dream or imagine!

In this devotion I want to challenge you to do a self-examination or *heart check*. I know how busy life is, and finding time for everything and everyone can be difficult. However, what about the widows, single moms and dads, or those around us who are struggling to even get out of bed in the mornings? Who will help them? Doesn't the Bible tell us it is our job to help those in need!

Let's make this personal. What are you doing for others outside of your immediate family? Have you considered mentoring or just sharing time with a child or teenager? What about a parent or guardian who could use some encouragement? If your response is, "I am just too busy!" Then maybe you should pray about your priorities and make some changes.

Every community has volunteer programs, and usually they are in need of reliable people. This is a great way to unselfishly reach out to others. If you are concerned about not having enough time with your own family, allow me to offer some advice. Set an example and take your kids along as often as possible. Show them the unselfish love of Christ in action by instilling this principle in their lives right now. It will make a positive and lasting impression, which will shape their present and future! If you have teenagers, require them to do some kind of volunteer work. We have personally experienced life-changing transformations in the young people God has blessed us with through the simple act of volunteering.

There is something so rewarding about helping someone without expecting anything in return, but I can assure you the return is truly great! It is filled with blessings, growth, and a life less selfish and self-absorbed. If this statement causes conviction, take heed and allow God to work in your heart in a new and wonderful way.

Let me ask you something, "Will you go to the next chapter and simply try to forget about these questions I have asked? Will you find every excuse possible to avoid praying and doing something about it?" Too late. The questions have been asked, and the challenge has been made! The rest is up to you.

I am praying for the Holy Spirit to begin a new work in hearts today, one that will cause a *rising up* and *reaching out* to others. It is time to roll up our sleeves and get a little dirty. We need to become a little uncomfortable and dare to live a life less selfish. Being overly consumed with *me, myself, and I*; along with things that have no eternal value, is not the way a Christian should choose to live!

There is no time like the present. Allow the following scriptures to speak to your heart. Don't be afraid of failing or making a mess of things. Lord knows, Bob and I make our share of mistakes! Through it all, we have learned to never stop reaching out to the lonely and those who are hurting. God will give you the strength and ability to become an extension of His love and make an eternal difference in the lives of others.

"Practice hospitality to one another (those of the household of faith). [Be hospitable, be a lover of strangers, with brotherly affection for the unknown guests, the foreigners, the poor, and all others who come your way who are of Christ's body.] And [in each instance] do it ungrudgingly (cordially and graciously, without complaining but as representing Him).

As each of you has received a gift (a particular spiritual talent, a gracious divine endowment), employ it for one another as [befits] good trustees of God's many-sided grace [faithful stewards of the [a]extremely diverse powers and gifts granted to Christians by unmerited favor]. (1 Peter 4:9-10, AMP)

"What good is it my brothers, if a man claims to have faith but has no deeds? Can such faith save him? Suppose a brother or sister is without clothes and daily food. If one of you says to him 'Go, I wish you well; keep warm and well fed,' but does nothing about his physical needs, what good is it? In the same way, faith by itself, if it is not accompanied by action, is dead." (James 2:14-17, NIV)

"In everything I did, I showed you that by this kind of hard work we must help the weak, remembering the words the Lord Jesus Himself said: 'It is more blessed to give than to receive.'" (Acts 20:35, NIV)

"For I mean not that other men be eased, and ye burdened: But by equality, that now at this time your abundance may be a supply for their want, that their abundance also may be a supply for your want; that there may be equality." (2 Corinthians 8:13-14, NIV)

"Be not forgetful to entertain strangers; for thereby some have entertained angels unawares." (Hebrews 13:2, NIV)

L–R: Mateo, Tamara and Kayla

L–R: Kayla, Mateo and Tamara

Chapter 15

Who Am I?

"Yet to all who received Him, to those who believed in His name, He gave the right to become Children of God." (John 1:12, NIV)

Scripture Focus

"Know that the Lord is God. It is He who made us, and we are His; we are His people, the sheep of His pasture." (Psalm 100:3-5, NIV)

"You made all the delicate, inner parts of my body and knit me together in my mother's womb. Thank you for making me so wonderfully complex! Your workmanship is marvelous—how well I know it. You watched me as I was being formed in utter seclusion, I was woven together in the dark of the womb. *You saw me before I was born. Every day of my life was recorded in Your book. Every moment was laid out before a single day had passed. How precious are Your thoughts about me, O God.* They cannot be numbered! I can't even count them; they outnumber the grains of sand! And when I wake up, *You are still with me!* (Psalm 139:13-18, NLT, emphasis added)

"I have loved you with an everlasting love; I have drawn you with loving-kindness." (Jeremiah 31:3, NIV)

"Lord, You have been our dwelling place throughout all generations. Before the mountains were born or You brought forth the earth and the world, from everlasting to everlasting *You are God.*" (Psalm 90:1-2, NIV, emphasis added)

This Is Who I Am!

By Dr. Donna Wilcox

I am a little girl who hates being sick.
God, please heal me.
I am a teenager struggling to understand why sickness plagues my life.
Why am I alive?
I am a Christian who believes in the gifts of salvation and healing.
God, where are you?
I am only nineteen years old and will never have children of my own.
I am sad.
Why am I here?
I am a confused young woman in my twenties. All I feel is pain.
Am I being punished?
I am in my early thirties; divorced and full of shame.
Can I ever be forgiven?
I am a woman with a past. Broken promises, poor choices, and painful memories.
God, please don't forsake me.
I am only thirty-five, scared and facing cancer.
I want to live!
I am a joyful woman in my late thirties who was not forsaken.
Thank you God!
I am a sinner saved by grace, and I am alive!
In Christ, I am healed and strong.
In Christ, I am happy and free.
In Christ, I am blessed and highly favored.
Because of Christ I am restored; I am a wife, missionary, and mother to many.
You are such a faithful Father!
Because of Christ I have a testimony that I shall never cease to tell.
Who am I? Oh, I know full well!
I am a King's daughter.
I am loved beyond measure and accepted just as I am.

Because of the blood of Jesus, I am the righteousness of Christ! This is who I am.

With all my shortcomings and imperfections; *this is who I am!*

~The End~

Truth

It took many years to finally start discovering who I am in Christ. As Believers, it is a process we all must go through. My journey of discovery continues, and every day God surprises me with a new revelation of His love for me, His daughter.

Oh how desperately I long to instill this truth into the young people the Lord has given us! I pray they never stop searching and asking questions. The most important thing we can do is continuously seek God's truth and what His Word says about our lives.

Parenting and working with young people has many rewards; however, it also has numerous challenges. The most common issues seem to center on the search for answers to some age-old questions, such as; "Who am I? What purpose do I have? Why am I here?" The answers can be hard to find. Especially if you spend your life looking in all the wrong places!

Dietrich Bonhöeffer was a young theologian born of great promise on February 4, 1906. He was condemned to death on April 8, 1945; and executed by hanging in the concentration camp at Flossenbürg on April 9, 1945. He was one of four members of his immediate family to die at the hands of the Nazi regime for their participation in the small Protestant Resistance Movement. It has been said, "The integrity of his Christian faith and life, and the international appeal of his writings, have led to a broad consensus that he is the one theologian of his time to lead future generations of Christians into the new millennium."

Bonhoeffer was a spiritual writer, a musician, and an author of fiction and poetry. His writings and his life have greatly influenced people. As I researched information about this man, I became intrigued and amazed. From a very young age he seemed to have grasped God's purpose for his life. While in prison he wrote a poem titled, "Who Am I," and it is written with such honesty, yet one cannot help but feel a sense of vulnerability. The last line of his poem says, "Whoever I am, Thou knowest, O God, I am Thine!" This is such a profound and powerful statement, because he realized no matter what he belonged to God! I would like to encourage you to research information on Dietrich Bonhöeffer's life and read his prison poems. They will truly bless and inspire you!

Bob and I desire for all the young people God has placed in our lives to know they are God's children and He is their Father (and a very good Father)! The greatest gift we can give these precious jewels is to simply point them toward the truth of God's infallible Word. This is where they will find the answers to life's questions, especially when they are seeking God for His will and purpose.

When it comes to seeking direction for our lives and our true purpose, opinions do not really matter. Submitting our will and desires to Jesus Christ will make the difference between success and failure.

Does this mean our desires and dreams are not important to God? No! He created us with certain desires, gifts, and talents for a reason. We are here to be God's instruments and walk in His blessings. In turn, we will experience joy and fulfillment. Our lives will overflow with the blessings of God and impact everyone we meet. In other words, we are blessed to be a blessing!

He has a good plan for all of us; however, it is up to us to seek Him for wisdom and direction. No one can or should do it for us! When we are focused on Christ we can walk in the confidence and determination needed to face the obstacles and challenges life throws our way; as we successfully pursue and fulfill our mission on earth.

I will leave you with a few important truths in your search for the answers to those questions that consume our thoughts and life. If you take heed, this information will change *how you think* and *what you choose to think and believe*. By finding out who you are in Christ Jesus our Lord, you will find the right path and fulfill absolutely everything you were created to do. The true meaning of happiness and success can be found in the following Scriptures.

I am God's child, John 1:12.
I am Christ's friend, John 15:15.

I am bought with a price, 1 Corinthians 6:19-20.
I am a personal witness of Christ, Acts 1:8.
I am the salt & light of the earth, Matthew 5:13-14.
I am a member of the Body of Christ, 1 Corinthians 12:27.
I am free forever from condemnation, Romans 8:1-2.
I am a citizen of Heaven. I am significant, Philippians 3:20.
I am free from any charge against me, Romans 8:31-34.
I am a minister of reconciliation for Christ, 2 Corinthians 5:17-21.
I have access to God through the Holy Spirit, Ephesians 2:18.
I am seated with Christ in the heavenly realms, Ephesians 2:6.
I cannot be separated from the love of God, Romans 8:35-39.
I am established, anointed, and sealed by God, 2 Corinthians 1:21-22.
I am assured all things work together for good, Romans 8:28.
I have been chosen and appointed to bear fruit, John 15:16.
I may approach God with freedom and confidence, Ephesians 3:12.
I can do all things through Christ who strengthens me, Philippians 4:13.
I am the branch of the true vine, a channel of His life, John 15:1-5.
I am God's temple, 1 Corinthians 3:16.
I am complete in Christ, Colossians 2:10.
I am hidden with Christ in God, Colossians 3:3.
I have been justified, Romans 5:1.
I am God's co-worker, 1 Corinthians 3:9; 2 Corinthians 6:1.
I am God's workmanship, Ephesians 2:10.
The good works God has instilled in me will fully come to pass, Philippians 1:5-6.
I have been redeemed and forgiven, Colossians 1:14.
I have been adopted as God's child, Ephesians 1:5; Romans 8:16-17.

As you spend time in prayer and meditation, ask Jesus for a revelation of who you are in Him. Boldly state, "I am complete in Christ, and I will fulfill my purpose on this earth for the glory of God. Everything I have need of or will ever need is in Jesus Christ my Lord and Savior. In and through Him I can do all things!"

Amen! So be it!

Chapter 16

Prayer Never Ceased!

"Pray without ceasing. In everything give thanks in all circumstances."
1 Thessalonians 5:17-18, KJV

Scripture Focus

"My intercessor is my friend as my eyes pour out tears to God; on behalf of a man he pleads with God as a man pleads for his friend." (Job 16:20-21, NIV)

"Therefore, He is able to save completely those who come to God through Him, because He always lives to intercede for them. Such a High Priest meets our need—one who is holy, blameless, pure, set apart from sinners, exalted above the Heavens." (Hebrews 7:25-26, NIV)

"In the same way, the Spirit helps us in our weakness. We do not know what we ought to pray for, but the Spirit Himself intercedes for us with groans that words cannot express. And He who searches the heart knows the mind of the Spirit, because the Spirit intercedes for the saints in accordance with God's will. And we know in all things God works for the good of those who love Him, who have been called according to His purpose." (Romans 8:26-28, NIV)

"No, in all these things we are more than conquerors through Him who loved us." (Romans 8:37, NIV)

People with Faith Prayed and Prayed!

By Tonya Robinson

October 11, 1999, is when trouble stepped into my life. Several months prior to this date, I began having severe chest pains and feeling extremely lethargic. During the day I worked as a customer service representative at a call center, and interestingly enough, throughout the workday I did not experience much discomfort. However, nighttime was a totally different story. After lying down for the evening, I would wake up in the middle of the night with excruciating chest pains. From the bed, I would go into the living room and pray, "Lord, please make the pain go away; it is so unbearable."

Working in a stressful environment, I just knew the pain must be related to job stress or from smoking. At the time, I smoked about one pack of Kool cigarettes a day. Nevertheless, I continued to smoke and work as I endured constant pain. Within a year's time I had had two trips to the emergency room. Doctors misdiagnosed me with pneumonia in my right lung and put me on the customary seven-day Z-pack treatment.

Almost a year to the date of my last emergency-room visit I sat at work no longer able to endure and ignore the tremendous pressure and intense pain in my chest. I got up from my workstation and went to make a telephone call to my doctor. I told the nurse what type of pain I was having, and she said that it sounded serious to her, and advised me to call 911. I did not want to alarm my co-workers by having an ambulance show up at work, so I drove myself back to the emergency room for the third time, with one hand gripping the steering wheel while holding on to what would be my last cigarette. Once again, I was misdiagnosed with pneumonia and sent home.

The following week I drove myself back to the doctor's office. This time he finally took an x-ray and a CBC (blood count) test. He found a mass on my right lung along with some other unexpected news. He said, "You are pregnant!" The news was so overwhelming the doctor told me to call my husband in to discuss the diagnosis. My husband (Rufus) and I were both inconsolable, and we began to pray. Being diagnosed with cancer is scary enough but to be pregnant at the same time was a double blow that we were not prepared for. We were absolutely heartbroken. How would this mass affect a baby?

My world seemed to be spiraling out of control. When I finally regained my composure, I suddenly realized something and told my doctor that I could not be pregnant, because I had a tubal ligation in June of 1999. This prompted him to take another look at the CBC blood count. Without much delay, he referred me to an oncologist and a surgeon.

"Weeping may endure for a night but joy cometh in the morning." (Psalm 30:5, KJV)

I was admitted to the hospital, where I underwent several test to confirm the cancer diagnosis. The test concluded that I was not pregnant, but I did have a rare cancer named cariocarcinoma. At the time there were only fourteen known cases in the United States. This cancer is the result of a dislodged placenta, which I found strange and unbelievable. Usually, the placenta reaches a certain phase and stops, but in those rare cases where the placenta does not stop growing women develop an aggressive and very serious cancer called cariocarcinoma.

After consulting with the surgeon, arrangements were made to schedule surgery as soon as possible to remove my right lung (pneumonectomy). On Wednesday, October 25 of 2000, God watched over me and guided the surgeon and his team through a successful operation. Prayer never ceased, and praise certainly accompanied the close of this chapter in my life.

Although I endured many hospital stays, chemotherapy treatments, and blood transfusions, God brought me through it all. I found comfort in His promise, "I will never leave you nor forsake you. I will be with you even to the end of time." My family and friends mobilized and began a prayer vigil. Prayer never ceased!

Three years passed, and everything seemed to be going well, or so I thought. In 2003 I became ill again, experiencing some of the same symptoms I had when diagnosed with cancer. Because of insurance issues, I was referred to an oncologist in Pensacola, Florida, which is about one hour away from home. After several tests, the doctors diagnosed me with leukemia, and they admitted to Baptist Hospital. My faith did not fail;

I trusted God to bring me through and heal me once again. Faced with another long series of intense treatments and even the possibility of a bone-marrow transplant, we prayed and trusted God. It was not always easy, but He gave me strength to carry on.

One of the side effects of the blood transfusions caused my whole body to swell up with fluid. At the same time, the left side of my body felt as though I had been badly burned. The pain was so severe I could not tolerate being touched, and nothing they tried brought relief. A team of doctors came in, puzzled and perplexed, because they did not understand my condition. They continued to do everything they knew to do to make me as comfortable as possible. I could not do anything but pray and trust God for divine healing.

Over a five-year period I never spent one night alone in the hospital. My family never left my side. They rotated in shifts, making sure I received the best care possible. I know for a fact that the love and support of my family and friends played a tremendous part in God's plan to heal me.

Family members know automatically what they are supposed to do when a crisis shows up unannounced and uninvited, but it is a little different with friends. From the very beginning of my illness, surgery, recovery, and healing, God blessed me with a few faithful friends that never ceased to pray for me.

In the beginning when I was first hospitalized, there were times when both my husband Rufus and my sister Sharona were overly protective. Following doctor's orders, they would screen my visitors. With my low blood counts, I was a prime candidate and a perfect target for any and all infections, so my bodyguards were there to protect me.

However, Donna would not be deterred! My dear friend and sister in Christ, Donna Wilcox, made sure that she saw me face to face. She did not take no for an answer. At the time of my first diagnosis and subsequent treatments she came to the hospital, pushing her way through with a scripture or two in hand. She was the only one from the call center my family allowed in at the hospital and when I arrived home after surgery. No place was off limits to her. I thank God for her persistence, and I value our lifelong friendship.

God did not stop with Donna; He also blessed me with Agnes Davis, Pat Sowell, Elaine Wilson, and many more that prayed for me, sent cards, and called to bless me during my days of recovery. Each of them continues to be very instrumental in my overall healing and well-being. Proverbs 18:24 states, "A man that hath friends must show himself friendly." Proverbs 17:17 also tell us, "A friend loveth at all times." I love my friends!

What have I learned from this journey? As I reread the chapters in my life before cancer, after several surgeries, and my life today, I know that God looked favorably upon me. I know that I am to be a living testimony to tell of His goodness and mercy. I am a two-time cancer survivor, and God expects me to share my testimony and life's story to bless and help others persevere who are facing this devastating disease.

Presently I volunteer with the leukemia Lymphoma Society, on call to offer moral support to newly diagnosed patients, as well as answering questions they may have on what to expect. I also encourage and pray for cancer patients within my family, friends, and community through a card ministry. What have I learned: to trust God in all things and never cease to pray!

"Confess your faults one to another, and pray one for another, that ye may be healed. The effectual fervent prayer of a righteous man availeth much." (James 5:16, KJV)

~ My Life…To Be Continued! ~

Truth

From the moment I met Tonya I knew we were going to be friends. We worked in a stressful atmosphere, full of quotas and ever-changing policies and requirements. Most of the people in the call center had worked for the phone company many years, and they were dealing with what happens when a small hometown company is taken over by a major corporation. New faces were everywhere along with new rules. I was one of those new faces.

The Lord gave me many wonderful friends during my days at the call center, and it has been an honor to put some of their stories in this devotional. I am thankful for their unselfish willingness to share God's blessings in their lives with others.

Shortly after beginning my new job, God divinely arranged for me and Tonya to sit next to one another. She is what we call in the South, *a hoot!* I love to laugh, and she was a comedy act without even trying. The call center didn't know what hit them when they put the two of us together! In spite of the hardships and stress, a lot of joy came from our little corner of the world.

Tonya had been with the company for many years, and I was the new girl. I knew in my heart the Lord wanted us to be friends but I did not make it easy. You see, every day I beamed with excitement about the new job opportunity the Lord provided through this corporation. *Being Donna*, I felt an intense desire to share my excitement with anyone willing to listen, not realizing the stress many people were experiencing due to the changes.

Bob and I just moved into our first new home together and my previous employer sold out to another company, drastically cutting everyone's pay. The call center offered me a position making more money than I had ever made, so this turned out to be a huge blessing! On the other hand, Tonya and many others were losing a small, close-knit family because of the changes.

Somehow, God gave Tonya a soft and receptive heart toward me. I excitedly shared my testimony about how the Lord healed me of cancer and the many blessings He brought into my life through the years. We both loved the Lord, and through this time of sharing and learning about one another our friendship grew.

During my cancer crisis the Word of God radically penetrated and changed my life, and I felt driven to share my miracle with others. I knew Tonya loved the Lord, and from the moment we began sitting next to one another I felt the Holy Spirit speak to me about giving her a scripture every morning. For some reason I could not ignore this persistent nudge.

Every day for about six months I arrived at work and handed her a hand written scripture. She always smiled, thanked me, and stopped to read it before putting it safely in her desk. Throughout the day, I noticed she often opened her desk drawer and read the scripture again. It felt wonderful sharing the Word this way with my new friend. Neither of us knew the strategic and divine nature of God's hand in our morning ritual. He was preparing and equipping us for the days that lay ahead by embedding His Word in our hearts and minds. Father God is clever, and there are no coincidences in His well-prepared plans!

Almost a year passed before Tonya's health crisis hit. I remember feeling devastated when I heard the news. My wonderful friend had been admitted to the hospital in critical condition and she needed a miracle. This was my sister, my friend. She had been coughing a lot due to what we thought was pneumonia; but not cancer! I simply refused to accept it!

I decided to have a long talk with God about the situation, and something strange and wonderful happened. I saw what looked like a movie screen in front of me, and there stood Tonya with me by her side. In the vision, I saw myself walk into the call center and hand her a scripture. The next scene unfolded with us laughing and talking about God's goodness. Suddenly, the picture disappeared and everything changed. Clearly and powerfully I heard God speak. His words went through me like an explosion inside my body; "Donna, I knew she would need you and the strength of your testimony. I am her Healer; My Word is true and faithful. It is what formed your friendship. My Word will not fail!"

A warrior-type spirit arose within my soul. It refused to back down no matter what! When Tonya says in her story I would not be deterred from seeing her, she wasn't kidding. I knew her family protectively stood guard and did not want visitors. I understood and appreciated their dedication to Tonya, but I was on a mission. I simply had to get to my friend and share the words God spoke to my heart!

I prayed they understood the urgency and my intense desire to see Tonya. I felt I must remind her of how God daily planted His Word in her spirit before this health crisis hit. With scriptures in hand I set out to get to my friend. I wanted to assure her our prayers would not cease until she received a miracle. Her family graciously and lovingly welcomed me, and I am forever grateful. They not only allowed me to see her but also treated me like part of their family.

Many people stood in prayer for Tonya. It unified those of us who were Christians in the call center, as well as non-believers. Churches were praying, friends and family prayed, we all prayed. We refused to waiver. We needed a miracle and that is what we asked for. Praise be to God, a miracle is what we got!

Tonya's healing was not an instantaneous event. As you read her story, she detailed the surgeries and hospital stays, along with the difficult treatments and so much more she courageously endured over a long period of time. The prayers of intercession by so many people turned out to be a powerful, life-changing miracle for all of us. It brought everyone together. We were focused and fearlessly willing to ask and believe God for a supernatural intervention of healing for our friend.

This kind of intercession is very common in the scriptures. One of my favorite Bible stories is about Aaron, Hur, and Moses. It is a beautiful example of the power of intercession.

The Amalekites attacked the Israelites while they were at Rephidim. Moses instructed Joshua to choose some men and go fight. Let's read what happened!

"As long as Moses held up the staff in his hand, the Israelites had the advantage. But whenever he dropped his hand, the Amalekites gained the advantage. Moses' arms soon became so tired he could no longer hold them up. So Aaron and Hur found a stone for him to sit on. Then they stood on each side of Moses, holding up his hands. So his hands held steady until sunset. As a result, Joshua overwhelmed the army of Amalek in battle." (Exodus 17:11-13 NLT)

These scriptures clearly teach us an important lesson; we need one another! Jesus Christ is the *Great Intercessor*, who is always interceding on our behalf. And He wants us to do the same for others.

Sometimes we face battles that are painfully hard and intense. We need our brothers and sisters to keep our arms lifted in faith toward Heaven. Like Moses experienced, this is where our strength comes from.

In closing, allow me to ask a few important questions. "Are you willing to be an Aaron or Hur? Are you willing to stand in the gap for a brother or sister who is in desperate need of a miracle?" If your answer is "Yes", ask God for wisdom and reach out to someone in need today.

Perhaps you are the one in need of intercessory prayer. If so, confess your need for prayer and allow people of faith into your life. This is not a sign of weakness. On the contrary! It is a step toward true faith in God's power to do the impossible. God responds to faith because it is the key to experiencing a growing, loving relationship with our Creator.

"And without faith it is impossible to please God, because anyone who comes to Him must believe that He exists and that He rewards those who earnestly seek Him." (Hebrews 11:6, NIV)

I love the scripture Tonya closed her story with, "Confess your faults one to another, and pray one for another, that ye may be healed. The effectual fervent prayer of a righteous man availeth much." (James 5:16, KJV). Confession and intercession leads to healing and deliverance. Father God is waiting. Take a step of faith toward healing and deliverance today!

Chapter 17

Stand, Strive, and Grow

"So then brothers, stand firm and hold to the teachings we passed on to you." (2 Thessalonians 2:15, NIV)

Scripture Focus

"So, if you think you are *standing firm*, be careful that you don't fall! No temptation has seized you except what is common to man. And God is faithful; He will not let you be tempted beyond what you can bear. But when you are tempted, He will also provide a way out so that you can *stand* up under it." (1 Corinthians 10:12-13, NIV, emphasis added)

"You too, be patient and *stand firm*, because the Lord's coming is near. Don't grumble against each other, brothers, or you will be judged. The Judge is standing at the door!" (James 5:8-9, NIV, emphasis added)

"Therefore, my dear brothers, *stand firm*. Let nothing move you. Always give yourselves fully to the work of the Lord, because you know that your labor in the Lord is not in vain." (1 Corinthians 15:58, NIV, emphasis added)

"Finally, be strong in the Lord and in His mighty power. Put on the full armor of God so that you can take your stand against the devil's schemes.... Therefore, put on the full armor of God, so that when the day of evil comes, you may be able to *stand* your ground, and after you have done everything, to *stand*. *Stand firm* then, with the belt of truth." (Ephesians 6:10-11, 13-14, NIV, emphasis added)

The Crooked Tree

By Debbie Wilcox

There is a pine tree in my backyard. You are probably thinking that there is nothing special about that fact. While this is true, not many people have a tree quite like this one. It is not a majestic pine towering above the rest, or an ancient tree to be admired for its beauty and stature. No. This tree is a crooked, twisted little tree that most people would not look at twice. This tree, however, is a very special tree that deserves a second look. You see, it carries a message from God.

Let me explain about this little tree. It does not talk. No leaflets or posters are attached to it. There are no profound words of wisdom carved deeply into its slender trunk. The message is not that apparent. To see the message clearly, you have to stop and look closely at the entire tree. This little pine tree is young and cannot be more than fifteen to twenty years old. In those years, many hurricanes hit our area, and the fact that this little pine tree is still standing is a testimony to its deep roots. The trunk is slender and appears to have been twisted and bent by the forces of those same hurricanes; yet that same trunk continues to grow always upwards.

While most pine trees have a single trunk much like a ship's mast, this little tree has a trunk with branches at the top like two arms raised high in praise to its Maker. A single pinecone hangs from one of its branches as a clear sign that this tree is fertile and producing seeds.

At this point, you may be scratching your head and wondering how I find a message from God in this crooked little tree. The message is this: stand. Stand and grow where God plants you. Read His Word, and apply it to your life so that you will be deeply rooted in it. When the evil forces of this world try to destroy you, you may bend and twist, but you will not break. God will protect and shape you into a new and even stronger person, a person with a testimony to share, and thus, seeds to plant.

My sincere prayer is that no matter how the forces of this world pull or push at me, I will always be in my Father's will. Always reaching upward, ever praising Him and striving each day to be a little closer to His glory. I have a pine tree in my backyard, and I want to be just like it.

~The End~

Truth

"The Crooked Tree" was written by my sister-in-law, Debbie Wilcox. I read it for the first time in 2006 when we returned from India and went home to Florida for a visit. With a beautiful simplicity, Debbie's story expressed the message of standing firm in God while growing and staying faithful in what we are called to do.

Bob has four younger brothers and two sisters, (one younger and one older). For many years we lived close to Bob's brother's Ron and Dennis; which made it easy to get to know them. In May of 2008, we visited Bob's hometown of Sparta, Wisconsin. During our visit, I spent time with his brother Rick and youngest sister, Eileen. My husband's family are all really good folks and I feel blessed to be a part of them.

In this devotion I want to focus on several things we all need to be reminded of from time to time. Yes, we must stand firm on the truth of God's Word, but just as important we should *grow*, *strive*, and *thrive* in our love walk with Jesus Christ and our fellow man.

As you reflect on the scriptures in the beginning of this devotion, the emphasis placed on standing firm is obviously an important part of our spiritual growth. The scriptures remind us of God's ability to deliver us from the enemy's schemes and the destructive lure of temptation. It also reminds us to give ourselves over to the work of the Lord, and not to waiver or move away from truth.

I personally love how 1 Corinthians 15:58 combines *standing* with *action*: "Stand firm. Let nothing move you. Always give yourselves fully to the work of the Lord, because you know that your labor in the Lord is not in vain."

We are to stand firm on the truth of God's Word while we are busy doing the work of the Father, always keeping in mind our labor is not in vain. Although this can be challenging at times, with the help of the Holy Spirit it is possible and filled with many rewards.

God knows our circumstances, and He is always at work on our behalf. Your situation may seem hopeless or out of control, but you can rest in the fact the Lord is faithful and true. He specializes in the impossible and will never leave or forsake His children. Miracles happen when we choose to place our complete faith and trust in Him.

Once you decide to do this, you must resist the enemy by standing firm on the truth of God's Word. In order to accomplish this task, it is important to know what is in God's Holy Word! As the wind blows and howls against us, another essential ingredient in achieving success and experiencing a breakthrough in the midst of the storm is *praise!*

Our job today and every day that we are blessed to walk on this earth is to be a light in the darkness, stay the course, and strive to do the Father's will. Like Debbie wrote, "Always reaching upward, ever praising our Maker."

Ephesians 6 gives us specific instructions on how to prepare for battle and receive victory. Below are some important points to meditate on:

1. We are to be strong in the Lord (not ourselves) and in His mighty power (not our own).
2. Put on the full armor of God. To do this we must be clothed with the belt of *Truth* buckled around our waist, the breastplate of *righteousness*, our feet fitted with *readiness*, taking up the shield of *faith*, the helmet of *salvation*, and the *sword of the Spirit*. Notice that each item listed is for our protection and to equip us for absolute victory when we are in battle!
3. Ephesians 6:18 offers another key ingredient, "Pray on all occasions with all kinds of prayer and requests. With this in mind, be alert and always keep on praying for all the saints." *Oh, sweet prayer, praise, and intercession!*

In closing, let us look at Ephesians 6:13-18 from the Amplified Bible. This translation will bring even more clarity as it places us in a position to *stand*, *strive*, and *grow*. Prayerfully ask the Holy Spirit to open your heart and mind to the complete and undeniable truth of God's Word. With stubborn persistence, decide to be like that crooked tree; determined to stand in faith against whatever comes your way!

"Therefore put on God's complete armor, that you may be able to resist and stand your ground on the evil day (of danger), and, having done all (the crisis demands), to stand (firmly in your place). Stand therefore, (hold your ground), having tightened the belt of truth around your loins and having put on the breastplate of integrity and of moral rectitude and right standing with God, And having shod your feet in preparation to face the enemy with the firm-footed stability, the promptness, and the readiness (produced by the Good News) of the Gospel of peace (Isaiah 52:7). Lift up over all the (covering) shield of saving faith, upon which you can quench all the flaming missiles of the wicked one. And take the helmet of salvation and the sword that the Spirit wields, which is the Word of God. Pray at all times (on every occasion, in every season) in the Spirit, with all (manner of) prayer and entreaty. To that end keep alert and watch with strong purpose and perseverance, interceding in behalf of all the saints (God's consecrated people)." (Ephesians 6:13-18, AMP)

Chapter 18

Persevering When There Seems to Be No Answer

"Let us hold fast the profession of our faith without wavering; (for He is faithful that promised)..." (Hebrews 10:23, KJV)

Scripture Focus

"And we rejoice in hope of the glory of God. Not only so, but we also rejoice in our sufferings, because we know that suffering produces perseverance; perseverance, character; and character, hope. And hope does not disappoint us, because God has poured out His love into our hearts by the Holy Spirit, who He has given us." (Romans 5:2-5, NIV)

"So do not throw away your confidence; it will be richly rewarded. You need to persevere so that when you have done the will of God, you will receive what He has promised. For in just a very little while, He who is coming will come and will not delay. But my righteous one will live by faith. And if he shrinks back, I will not be pleased with him. *But we are not of those who shrink back and are destroyed, but of those who believe and are saved.*" (Hebrews 10:35-39, NIV, emphasis added)

Rachel's Horrible Headaches

By Rachel Heaner

"My head hurts all the time, Mom. It never stops." It was October 1994. I was ten years old, and my head constantly hurt. It hurt when I sat up, stood, or lay down. We could not figure out the cause of this horrible headache that would not go away. I had not fallen nor hit my head. The area a baseball cap would cover is where it hurt the most.

Mom and I prayed every day and asked many people to pray for me, too. Mom decided to take me to a pediatrician, but he could not pinpoint the cause of my headache. He prescribed some medication to help with the pain, but the medicine did not make the headache go away. We read Bible verses about God's power to heal, and Mom even took me to a healing center for prayer; however, the headache continued, all day every day.

Eventually a pediatric neurologist examined me and ordered multiple tests, but each one came back normal. They had no success in figuring out the cause of this ongoing, painful headache.

"God loves you, Rachel," Mom told me over and over. "He knows what is causing your headache, even if the doctors don't. He is caring for you."

My eyes brimmed with tears as I thought; *My head hurts so much. Why won't this headache go away?* The previous four months had felt like one long, world-record headache.

Mom came up with a "headache scale" to help me describe my pain. "One" meant minimal pain; "ten" meant excruciating pain. "My head hurts more than a ten!" I cried. I longed for the pain to go away. I wanted to be able to run and play with my friends and brothers again, without having to deal with this horrible headache.

A few weeks later, after an appointment with a Christian chiropractor, my head hurt a little bit less. After my next chiropractor visit, my headache lessened to a "seven" on the headache scale. Each day the pain decreased. Finally, on February 7, 1995, God healed me. My headache was totally gone! After four months of constant pain, God healed me completely!

We held a praise party with friends and family who had prayed for me. We went out for pizza, and returned home to sing our favorite praise songs to God. Mom helped me write down my story, and I shared my testimony at church on the following Sunday.

Six months later, in August 1995, I got another horrible headache. I thought, *Oh no! How long will this one last?* In my 11-year-old mind, I wondered if this one would also last for four months. I did not want it to, but that thought kept creeping into my mind. Mom and I prayed so many times, asking God to take this headache away. God healed me of my four-month-long headache, so I knew He was able to heal me of this new one.

My head continued to hurt all of the time, during the autumn months, over Thanksgiving, and throughout the Christmas holidays. All winter long my head ached continually. It was hard to persevere in prayer because of the pain. We were not seeing our prayers change anything, so we began to pray and thank God in advance for the healing He would provide.

"I'm not sure my headache will ever go away," I confided to Mom, "but God healed me before and He can do it again."

Twenty-four hours a day, seven days a week, my headache plagued me constantly for eleven long and painful months.

One July afternoon, while riding in the car with mom, I exclaimed, "Mom, my headache is only a seven on the headache scale!" Before we got home, it was a three. Later that day I shouted, "My headache is gone! It's totally gone!" My eyes sparkled, and my countenance beamed as I romped around the house giving praise. "Thank you for healing me, God! It's so good to be rid of that horrible headache!"

My family and I hugged and together praised God.

I told my friends, "God built my trust in Him through the troubling times with my horrible headaches. God has perfect timing in every situation. Whether you know it or not, He is caring for you all of the time."

Since God healed me of my second horrible headache in 1995, I have not had a problem with ongoing headaches. We never did find out the cause of them, but throughout those pain-filled days as a ten- and eleven-year-old, I learned a lot about trusting God and persevering in prayer. Even when I do not understand why He does not answer prayers right away, I have come to realize God's timing is best.

~The End~

Truth

Bob and I are so blessed to have young people like Rachel in our lives. She is one of the most faithful young women of God we know. When I think about Rachel, I think about character and integrity. She is such a pure and beautiful example of the scripture, "…because we know that suffering produces perseverance; perseverance, character; and character, hope." Reading her story brought a genuine sense of joy to my spirit. At the tender age of ten and eleven, she was able to put her faith in God and wait until the answer came.

How many of us would have persevered with this kind of patience and determination Rachel so wonderfully demonstrated? God's Word is clear on the subject of giving up or shrinking back: "But my righteous one will live by faith. And if he shrinks back, I will not be pleased with him. But we are not of those who shrink back and are destroyed, but of those who believe and are saved" (Hebrews 10:38-39, NIV).

These scriptures never say we have permission to give up and stop believing if our prayers are not quickly answered. Quite the contrary! God tells us He will not be pleased with that kind of attitude. Is this easy? No! The only way to accomplish this challenging task is to *feed your faith* with the Word, and *purpose in your heart to hold out and hold on* until the answer comes. Some of my greatest victories took years to manifest. When the answer finally arrived, I could see how God used that time to gently draw me into a closer relationship with Him and bring wisdom into my life.

Many people turn away from the Lord because they feel He did not answer their prayers when and how they thought He should. This is not faith. In fact, it is the complete opposite. It is as if we are saying, "Okay, God, I will believe in You as long as You prove Yourself to me." How this must hurt the heart of our Father. He loves us so much He sent His One and Only Son to die on a cruel cross so that we may be saved, healed, and blessed beyond comprehension!

If you struggle with this kind of thinking, take a lesson from a young girl who dared to believe and stuck it out until her prayers were answered. This kind of love relationship with Jesus Christ is always rewarded.

Trusting God is truly a faith thing. He does answer prayer. And yes, sometimes it takes a little while to receive the answer.

I can assure you of one thing, He is an on-time God who is faithful and true. Do not allow discouragement to take up residence in your heart. Get in the Word and with perseverance hold on. Begin diligently setting aside time to praise the Lord for His love and mercy, then patiently wait for your miracle to manifest. Like Rachel, you will also have a testimony of His amazing power!

Our Rachel is a missionary with Youth with a Mission. She faithfully sows into the lives of young missionaries, taking them on outreaches to some of the most unreached areas of the world. Rachel is a gifted musician, and she truly is the hands, feet, and mouth of Christ. We are proud of her dedication to the things of God and her love walk with Jesus.

To know more about her ministry or how to contribute to her work, please contact me through my website: http://www.donnawilcox.com. You will be blessed, and your prayers and financial support will be greatly appreciated!

Chapter 19

Mad in Mexico

"Be not hasty in thy spirit to be angry: For anger resteth in the bosom of fools." (Ecclesiastes 7:9, KJV)

Scripture Focus

"In your anger do not sin. Do not let the sun go down while you are still angry, and do not give the devil a foothold."

"Get rid of all bitterness, rage and anger, brawling and slander, along with every form of malice. Be kind one to another, forgiving each other, just as in Christ God forgave you." (Ephesians 4:26-27, 31-32, NIV)

"Make every effort to live in peace with all men and to be holy, without holiness no one will see the Lord. See to it that no one misses the grace of God and that no bitter root grows up to cause trouble and defile many." (Hebrews 12:14-15, NIV)

I'm Mad, and I Have a Right to be!

By Dr. Donna Wilcox

It is hard to *do right* when you are mad! Especially if someone has been unkind or unjust for no apparent reason. Most people think Southern women are tactful, graceful, and polite. Obviously, they have never seen one have a *good ole fashion* "hissy fit." Given the right circumstances, we ain't so tactful, graceful or polite! I found myself in this very situation several years ago while doing missions work in Mexico.

You are probably thinking things like that shouldn't happen in missions or ministry. It shouldn't, and I am sorry to disappoint you but it does! Regardless of our profession, we are human and everyone makes mistakes. Unfortunately, no one is exempt. During this period in our ministry I faced one of the hardest challenges of my life and found out just how difficult it is to keep your tongue from evil and your temper in check. But it taught me a lesson I will never forget and always be grateful for.

We were scheduled to go to India in December of 2003, but at the last minute the base director asked us to go to a village in Central Mexico. Bob's building expertise was needed to help with the completion of a leadership school dormitory. They had faced numerous delays and problems getting the building completed, and over three hundred missionaries were scheduled to arrive in just a few months. The situation was critical because the students and their families needed adequate housing while they were in school.

We said our goodbyes to the India team and headed off (by ourselves) to Mexico. We had only been in missions about three months, and that time was spent in the classroom. We were a little nervous to say the least. Regardless, I knew this detour was an answer to a specific prayer I prayed before leaving for missionary school. You see, I am the outgoing one who never meets a stranger; however, Bob is shy and an introvert. I did not want him to get pushed in the background, so I asked God to allow Bob's gifts and talents to be recognized and used for His glory. The Lord heard my prayer, which turned out to be the reason for this sudden change of plans.

Bob went right to work when we arrived in Mexico. The work was physically hard and consisted of long hours with very little rest. On top of that, everyone we dealt with spoke Spanish and very little English. Neither of us spoke fluent Spanish. We actually only knew a few words and sentences. So Bob's challenges grew increasingly difficult. The first few weeks I helped him paint, go for this and that, and take snacks to the workers. Taking treats to everyone became the highlight of my day, and there weren't many highlights!

After I spent a few weeks helping Bob, the leader's wife decided to make a daily list of chores for me to do. We were there to serve so I happily took the list, determined to do such a good job that we would become fast friends. Unfortunately, I discovered something very unsettling; the leader's wife did not like me and I was about to find out what Cinderella felt like! Let me explain this statement. She had four young women doing the chores she gave me to complete on a daily basis and she wanted me to work completely alone. Even if I worked nonstop I could not have finished the daily list of chores. The young Mexican women were sweet, and they did not understand why I was suddenly doing all their work without any help. Before they could ask too many questions, she quickly sent them to the other side of the base with a new list of daily chores to keep them very busy.

For a social extrovert this proved devastating. I wanted to fellowship and make friends. Instead, I spent the majority of my days alone; mopping and sweeping, cleaning bathrooms, doing laundry, and kitchen duty. Like I said, I became Cinderella minus the evil stepsisters. That seemed to be the only silver lining!

I enjoyed kitchen duty and taking snacks to the workers. Taking snacks around to everyone just happened to be my idea, and I refused to let anything keep me from spreading a little good cheer, not to mention it gave me the opportunity to socialize! Everyone worked hard, and I knew they looked forward to these little breaks.

Edgar and Ethel ran the kitchen. They cooked all the meals and purchased the groceries. Edgar became a missionary shortly after becoming a Christian. He dreamed of spreading the love of God to his people. Ethel's family made a decision to go to missionary school together and serve on the base. She was a retired nurse and wore many hats. Ethel was a wife, mother of two teenage girls, managed the base kitchen, and was a friend to many. Ethel's husband had been an engineer in Mexico for a number of years, and he worked on the building project with Bob. Even though we faced a language barrier, through interpreters and charades they became very dear friends.

Spending time with Edgar and Ethel always filled my day with joy and laughter. We grew very close, and I loved and respected them tremendously. They worked hard from sun up to sundown, but you never heard them complain. I should have paid closer attention to this and tried to be more like them!

Technically, Bob was my Team Leader on this outreach. I went to him in tears unable to understand why the leader's wife treated me so badly, or what I had done to make her dislike me. I only complained to Bob because I wanted to be careful and respectful toward her as a leader, and not cause any problems on the base between the staff and students. Although he could not understand why she disliked me, he had his hands full trying to build a dormitory with people who spoke in a different language. My problems seemed small compared to what he faced every day. Anyway, we were there to serve and we knew missions work would not be an easy road. He lovingly listened and prayed, all the while believing things would improve once she got to know me.

In the midst of this God gave us another wonderful friend named Andy. He was from Germany and on staff at the base. Gifted like Bob, Andy could build, repair, and fix anything. He became our interpreter, which created many comical and confusing conversations. Andy interpreted Spanish with a thick German accent; thank God for charades! When I tried to speak Spanish everyone laughed, so I obviously did not speak correctly. I taught Ethel and Edgar some English words, and they taught me a little Spanish. I think they just wanted a good chuckle, and we sure enjoyed laughing together.

During the months we were there, missionary teams came from the States to help with the building project. No matter how hard the leader's wife tried to keep me isolated and busy, young people seemed to find their way to me. We were able to pray together, share testimonies, and keep each other encouraged. We witnessed answered prayer and healings during these times of fellowship God so divinely arranged. Unfortunately, it did not make me any less mad about the situation.

Christmas came and all the workers, students, and staff left to visit family and friends. The base director, his wife, and two children lived in a house on the property at the top of the hill. They invited us over for one meal and kept to themselves the rest of the time; however, the children were always sweet and friendly. Bob and I were essentially alone and we spent the days painting. The leaders locked the room that had the phone in it, so calling home to family in the States proved challenging. We did not have a car and since the base was far from the city, transportation in the middle of nowhere was next to impossible. The leaders also closed the main kitchen during the holidays, so when it came time to eat we went to a small staff's kitchen which contained very little food. We cooked whatever we could find. With each passing day we felt more like outcasts. It was very depressing.

Our difficulties in Mexico seemed bad enough, but something else troubled my mind. Right before leaving Florida in August of 2003, I saw this tiny red spot on my left cheek. I thought it might simply be a small pimple or bump. I really did not think too much about it. When I applied blush it stood out a little, so I dabbed it with a cover stick to blend it in with my makeup and take away the redness. When we started school in September it was still there, and just never went away. When December rolled around and we headed to Mexico, the bump changed. It began stinging and burning every morning as I applied makeup. So there we were, feeling unwanted in Mexico, alone at Christmas, and on top of everything else I had this irritating little spot on my face.

We finally made it through the holidays, and life resumed its normal busyness. My anger continued to grow a little more each day, and sadly, bitterness soon took root in my heart. Poor Bob came to our room at night after working so hard and had to put up with my rants about this mean woman who refused to like me regardless of how hard I tried. He finally had endured enough, and in total exhaustion he said, "Baby, the last thing you want to have to do is apologize to her because of the bitterness in your heart."

I could not believe it. Me? Bitter? No way! I quickly stated I wasn't bitter, just mad and had every right to be. With that, Bob quit talking about it and I did too.

That night we crawled in bed and lay in silence. Both of us were worn out from another day of work and struggling. Before drifting off to sleep I began praying for God to heal the spot on my cheek. Immediately something happened that humbled me in such a profound way.

God spoke directly to my heart and this is what I heard, "Donna, I cannot heal you until you forgive."

I began crying and asking God to forgive me for the anger and bitterness in my heart. I then started praying for this woman, asking God to bless her. For the first time I felt a great compassion for her as I prayed. Then, it happened. As I wiped the tears from my eyes the red thing on my cheek fell off, right in my hand! I turned on the light to show Bob and apologized for everything I put him through. We rejoiced together, thankful for God's mercy and forgiveness.

The remainder of our time in Mexico continued to be hard, but peace and joy ruled in our hearts. We experienced the blessings and favor of God on a daily basis. The leader's wife did not change, but I certainly did. I went about my chores happy and praising God. Every time ugly thoughts entered my mind, I immediately stopped and rebuked those thoughts and prayed for this woman and her family. I felt free, no longer a slave to bitterness and anger. God also began giving me insight and revelation about the problem, which helped tremendously during my daily prayer walks around the base. In the name of Jesus, I prayed for His blood to cover and protect everyone there, and I bound the spirit of the enemy and his divisive plans. Prayer time became exciting and powerful!

"I will give you the keys of the Kingdom of Heaven; and whatever you bind (declare to be improper and unlawful) on earth must be what is already bound in Heaven; and whatever you (declare lawful) on earth must be what is already loosed in Heaven." (Matthew 16:19, AMP)

People continued to find their way to me for fellowship and prayer. Ethel and Edgar even threw a surprise birthday party for me with cake, balloons, and beautiful cards and letters from the staff and students. The Lord did not allow me to be kept isolated and alone. It was truly amazing to witness God in action!

Before leaving Bob bought all the workers a Youth with a Mission tee shirt and gave them a Bible in their language. He did not want to leave without testifying and giving praise to God. With the help of an Interpreter, he called the workers together and shared what was on his heart. He explained in detail the purpose of the building they labored so hard over to complete. They were grateful, and I felt so proud of Bob. God beautifully answered my prayer to use him for His glory in a mighty way and allow his gifts and talents to shine!

Leaving Mexico proved to be bittersweet. We were happy to get away from the situation but had fallen in love with the people. God gave us some dear friends that we would miss terribly. I am thankful for the valuable lessons God taught me during our time there. It brought wisdom into my Christian walk that continues to be a part of my life today.

When you are hurt or mad just remember, "In your anger do not sin." This is not always as easy as it sounds, and the enemy is very cunning. He is continuously looking for an opportunity to gain a foothold. One last pearl of wisdom: A daily *heart check* is vitally important when it comes to avoiding a root of bitterness. If you find one growing, humble yourself and repent!

~The End~

Truth

This story revealed an area of my heart that had grown very ugly, and I am ashamed of how I allowed anger to turn into something as dangerous as a root of bitterness. My prayer in sharing this is quite simple. I pray you will allow God to shine a light on any areas of unforgiveness and anger you may be harboring, and learn the power and freedom forgiveness brings.

You may be going through something similar. Someone has hurt you or caused pain in your life through no fault of your own. Yes, you have a right to be angry, but be careful! Anger can easily turn into bitterness. Once this happens it sends you spiraling down a path filled with negative and harmful emotions and thoughts, along with depression and the absence of blessings.

If you are praying for something and have not received an answer, examine your heart. Make sure you are not harboring a bitter root that is preventing God from answering your prayers. If the Holy Spirit brings something to mind, simply repent and ask the Lord for wisdom in dealing with the issue. He is faithful and just, and He hears the prayers of His children.

You may ask, "How will I know if the bitter root has gone, and I am forgiven?" Trust me, you will know! It does not mean you won't be angry. It also doesn't mean you will feel a mushy kind of love for those who have hurt you; however, you will feel peace and a desire to pray for the very one who has caused you pain.

Usually we notice the change within our own heart, not the one (or ones) who have wronged us. We cannot make others change their behavior, but we have the power to choose well and heed the Word of God for ourselves. By doing so, we will experience a restored peace and joy. It breathes life back into everyday living and wisdom in our love walk between God and man.

The truth is this; when we do not forgive and choose to remain bitter, *the person we are angry with controls our very life!* We also give the enemy a huge open door of destruction, as we begin walking a dangerous path.

There is an old saying, "Let go, and let God," and now is the time to do that very thing. *Let go* of the pain and hurt that has caused bitterness to take root, and *let God* bring healing to your heart. Only He can restore the joy back into your life. It is your choice. The decision you make will affect every aspect of your existence, so choose well!

Chapter 20

Praise to Jesu Cristo from Kenya!

"Sing to God, sing praise to His name, extol Him who rides on the clouds, His name is the Lord, and rejoice before Him. A father to the fatherless, a defender of widows, is God in His holy dwelling. *God sets the lonely in families;* He leads forth the prisoners with singing." (Psalm 68:4-6, NIV, emphasis added)

Scripture Focus

"For the Lord your God is God of gods, and Lord of lords, the great God, mighty and awesome, who shows no partiality and accepts no bribes. He defends the cause of the fatherless and the widow, and loves the alien, giving him food and clothing." (Deuteronomy 10:17-18, NIV)

"Defend the cause of the weak and fatherless; maintain the rights of the poor and oppressed. Rescue the weak and needy; deliver them from the hand of the wicked." (Psalm 82:3-4, NIV)

A Message of Love from Kenya

By Cori Fancher

I joined Youth With A Mission (YWAM) in 2003, along with my two-year-old daughter Hannah. I completed the Discipleship Training School (DTS) and then went on a two-month outreach to serve at a mission's base in Kenya. Hannah and I went with a team of YWAM students and staff. There were seventeen of us, including five children, all under the age of six years old.

I had only been out of the country once before, and this was the first time for Hannah. We stayed on the base in a small village called Mbita, on Lake Victoria. Even though they had dormitories, most of our team chose to sleep in tents on the beach of Lake Victoria, and that is where we lived for six weeks. I can remember Hannah saying, "Mommy, is this our new home?" The last two weeks of the outreach we moved to the dormitories because red ants began invading our tent.

As I look back on our first trip to Kenya, I believe God was showing us His heart for the children in that country. There are so many children in need, and many of them are without parents. They have to provide for themselves, and most of the older children are the caretakers of the younger ones. As we walked through the dusty dirt road of the village, the children looked so hopeless.

Hannah has blonde hair and beautiful blue eyes, and the children were drawn to her. When they ran up to see her, I felt as though I could see the joy of the Lord in their sweet faces. I put Hannah in a small stroller I brought with me for the long walks from the village to the YWAM base, and as the children crowded around to see her she would lift up her hand like a princess, to wave and shout, "Hey guys!" They all laughed and smiled. I loved seeing their smiles!

Our team had the opportunity to teach a Sunday school class of children ages five to twelve years old. As we were teaching them, I noticed a little girl about eight years old that had a big open wound on the top of her head with puss coming out of it. After we taught the children most of them left the classroom, but this little girl stayed. I knew that God wanted us to pray for her, so I asked if we could pray for her, and she nodded, *yes.* After we prayed she left without saying anything.

About a week later we were helping out at Christ's Gift Academy, a school that YWAM started for the orphans. As I passed out the morning porridge, I recognized one of the children. It was the little girl with the head wound that we prayed for in Sunday School. I felt relieved to see her again. I instantly looked at the top of her head, and it was totally normal. In less than a week her hair had even grown back. We had witnessed a miracle!

The people in Kenya have a simple lifestyle with very primitive living conditions. Yet, it really impressed me when we were attending one of their four-hour-long church services, because they freely and cheerfully gave in the offering. When the pastor said, it's time to give tithes and offerings, the people got up and started dancing down the aisles of the church to bring their small amount of coins. We Americans could learn something from these precious Kenyans!

Approximately five weeks into our stay we traveled to Mfangano Island on Lake Victoria. Researchers say that about 80 percent of the people living there are HIV positive. There were so many orphaned children on this island it was truly heartbreaking. We were housed at a boarding school for orphans and stayed in the girl's dorm. I have always had a deep desire to be given the opportunity to tuck orphans into bed and tell them that Jesus loves them, and God answered my prayer by letting me do this with about fifty girls at the boarding school. God is good!

While we were staying on this island we traveled by boat to a smaller island during the day to speak to the people there. The boat was scheduled to pick us up by 6 p.m. to bring us back to Mfangano Island. We waited and waited on the beach for hours, and it finally came about 10:00 p.m. It had taken so long we were worried, because we were all very hungry and had nowhere to sleep. As the community boat docked, we could see that it was way over its capacity, but we trusted God and went aboard.

The waves were big that night, and the boat rocked from side to side. Hannah and I were in the middle, and I watched the water rise up the sides of the boat. I would have to say this proved to be the most frightening time during our trip, but God stayed with us. As we started out in the water, the Africans in the boat started singing a song in Swahili to *Jesu Cristo* (Jesus Christ). I did not understand all the words, but I could feel God's peace as we went along. The moon hovered over the water, and it glowed with a brilliant orange and red. We sensed God's amazing love and protection!

Feeling a strong desire to go back after our outreach, Hannah and I returned to Kenya in 2005 for two more months. As we saw and heard more of their everyday life, this trip gave me a clearer reality of life in Kenya. We saw baby caskets attached to bicycles, and there were many nights we were awakened by very loud music and wailing, which I found out later was a funeral. Their tradition is to mourn and play loud music throughout the village whenever someone dies, and about every third day we heard these anguished sounds of pain and loss.

During this trip I heard the story of three orphaned children that were living with their grandmother. They had to provide and take care of her even though she often beat them. Then I talked with a twenty-three-year-old woman who was involved in prostitution because her mother needed a way to feed her five siblings. I heard story after story of pain, abuse, and hopelessness.

Through both of our trips to Kenya, God showed me that He came into a hurting world, and our only hope is in Him. He showed me that He truly is the Father to the fatherless. He cares for all His precious creations, and they are beautifully made in His image and likeness. He taught me a valuable lesson; even though it seems hopeless and there is so much despair, there is life in Him!

As you think of Kenya, please pray for the children. Pray that God would give them strength to rise up and live Godly, righteous lives. Pray that missionaries will continue to answer the call to "go" and share the message of love and hope.

~The End~

Truth

We are so blessed to have Cori and Hannah as part of our family, and we are proud of the work they accomplished in Kenya. Hannah is such a pretty little girl and an extremely loving child. It is through this relationship Bob and I learned the joy of being grandparents!

When Cori shared stories with us from their days in Kenya, we could just picture Hannah riding in the stroller and waving at everyone as she shouted out, "Hey guys!" That's our little Hannah—personality and then some! I could also see Cori's heart; so broken, yet full of love for the orphaned children as she lovingly tucked them into bed at night and made sure they knew Jesus loved them!

Not being able to return to Kenya has been difficult for Cori, but God had a different path for her and Hannah to go down. One thing is for sure; they will both continue to pray for the children of Kenya, and intercession is a powerful thing!

I love this story because it portrays the life of a single mother willing to be obedient to God, even if it meant going to a hard place with a toddler. That takes guts and determination! Their accomplishments and hard work in Kenya have eternal value, and God is moving mightily in that country because of people like them. I admire Cori tremendously, as do so many who know her and Hannah. She recently graduated from college and is a school teacher in Colorado, embarking on a brand new mission field!

I hope this story continues to spark something in your heart toward missions. There is no excuse not to answer the call to go. You may not be able to go in the physical sense; however, if you can it will change your life forever.

There are also other ways to *go* and participate. You can help send someone else who has a burning desire and call on their life to spread Jesus to the world! There are numerous ways to sow into ministries and missions: Through prayer, finances, or even care packages to front-line missionaries.

Seek God for direction, and find a way to reach out. As I expressed in previous chapters, this is an issue *all* Believers should be doing something about. We must *go, work,* and *do* while we can. The time is now!

"Do you not say, 'Four months more and then the harvest?' I tell you, open your eyes and look at the fields! They are ripe for harvest." (John 4:35, NIV)

Hannah and her friends from Kenya

Cori and Hannah

Chapter 21

Why We Struggle

"I will instruct you and teach you in the way you should go; I will counsel you and watch over you." (Psalm 32:8, NIV)

Scripture Focus

"Trust in the Lord with all your heart and lean not on your own understanding; in all your ways acknowledge Him, and He will make your paths straight." (Proverbs 3:5-6, NIV)

"For the Lord God is a sun and shield; the Lord will give grace and glory; no good thing will He withhold from them that walk uprightly. O Lord of hosts, blessed is the man that trusteth in Thee." (Psalm 84:11-12, KJV)

"Therefore, take no thought, saying, 'What shall we eat? or, What shall we drink? or, Wherewithal shall we be clothed?'…For your heavenly Father knoweth that ye have need of all these things." (Matthew 6:31-32, KJV)

I'm Listening Lord, but I'm Not Hearing Anything!

By Dr. Donna Wilcox

For years people who knew about my life and the obstacles I overcame often commented, "Donna, you should write a book. It could help a lot of people going through tough times." I usually laughed and came back with something smart like, "Yeah, but who would believe anyone could survive the life I've had and not be completely crazy?" I truly never gave it a moment's thought. I felt happy just to be alive and well.

One day something happened that changed my mind. After sharing my testimony with a young woman at work she decided to ask Jesus into her heart. When I arrived home that evening, I excitedly told Bob what happened. Before going to sleep, we prayed together for God's blessings her life. In the wee hours of the morning I suddenly woke up and heard something so deep and loud in my spirit it startled me. "Donna, write your life's story. Write it as if you are sharing your testimony with someone. Write in truth and love, and I will take care of the rest."

I did not know what to do or even how to respond. I continued praying, and once again the Lord spoke to my heart. The words felt like a boom inside my soul. "Write in truth and love, and I will take care of the rest." My first thought was; *What a relief. God is going to help me!* You see, God does not ask us to do something and disappear. He is a constant presence in our life. The Holy Spirit dwells within us and is always leading and directing our steps, but we must stay *tuned in* so that we can *hear Him.*

Several days passed and I still lacked the courage to tell Bob. I wondered what he would say when I hit him with this bombshell! I had never written a book and was completely clueless about the process, but more than anything I desired to be obedient.

I have learned to carefully listen to the voice of God when He speaks to my heart. It is truly unlike any sound I have ever heard. It is clear and precise and seems to penetrate through every cell of my being. Many people do not believe the Lord speaks to His children today, but I am so thankful He still does. Hebrews 13:8 tells us, "*Jesus Christ is the same yesterday, today, and forever.* Simply put; His voice has not grown silent!

An entire week passed and I continued to pray for God's strength and timing on when to tell Bob. It wasn't long before the opportunity arrived. One afternoon Bob came to the call center to take me to lunch. As we sat talking, tears suddenly streamed down my face and I blurted it out. Bob immediately began encouraging me to be obedient and start writing. I beamed with excitement knowing I had his approval. After drying my tears, I kissed Bob bye and headed back to work. It felt like a weight had been lifted off my shoulders; and little did I know that was just the beginning. Arriving home that night I walked into the kitchen and saw a laptop computer and a Bible disk sitting on the counter. Bob bought it that very afternoon, just for me. I am truly blessed! It means so much to a man or woman when their mates are supportive of their dreams and desires.

Before long, the process of writing began. If anyone tells you writing a book is easy, they are sadly mistaken! Writing is many things, but easy is not one of them. However, it did prove to be very therapeutic. So much happened in my life, some of which I never allowed myself to work through. Writing out every little detail proved to be an effective tool in the healing process. I lost all control as the Lord and I shared some intense conversations. The healing that occurred from these times of desperation and prayer felt like a cleansing river washing through every part of my body, including my mind! Looking back, it became apparent how faithful and loving God had been.

Although writing down every detail of my life proved to be beneficial in the healing process, it did not necessarily need to be published. After a lot of prayer and seeking God for wisdom, several things were deleted before submitting the final draft to the publisher.

For years I carried a secret and very few people in my life knew about it. After a lifelong battle with sickness and pain, I also became a victim of abuse when I was in my early twenties. My mom and dad were devastated and wanted to fight for me in every way possible, but only God can make the crooked paths straight and bring justice to our cause. It is better left in His hands. Like it or not God doesn't just love the victims, He also loves the abusers! I may not understand this kind of unconditional love and compassion, but I choose to trust the Lord. Doubting or questioning His mercy and wisdom is simply not an option for me. My parents respected my wishes, although I could see the hurt in their eyes due to feeling helpless in the situation.

Usually people who cause pain or harm to others have also been deeply hurt, and this is why they react in negative and damaging ways. I am not trying to justify wrong actions; this is just a fact. The truth is, when we have been unjustly hurt we cannot erase the scars or the memories and make them somehow disappear. Forgiveness is critical in the healing process, and if you profess to be a Christian there is no way around it. We are to obey God's commands without exception. God's Word clearly tells us if we do not forgive He will not forgive us when we sin. It is our choice and if we choose well blessings will come forth from our obedience. I made my decision, and the freedom that followed was nothing short of miraculous.

Throughout the writing process, the Holy Spirit meticulously and lovingly brought healing to those wounds. To publish the details would have been a way of seeking revenge or to gain some kind of personal satisfaction. The truth is, I received an amazing gift. My Heavenly Father gave me the ability to forgive! God doesn't do anything halfway. He miraculously performed heart surgery as he mended what felt like a lifetime of pain and hurt.

Several years passed, and I finally completed the book. The task had been both difficult and wonderful, but now the time had come to do something with it. I sought God for wisdom as I began searching for Christian publishers who accepted autobiographies. I made a list and prayed over it, then began getting my manuscript ready to be sent out. Bob and I were scheduled to leave for vacation in just a few weeks to go skiing in Colorado. I made a promise to God to have my book together and in the mail before leaving. Little did I know just how difficult that promise would be to keep!

The closer time grew for us to leave on our ski trip the more disorganized I became. I researched a few things about how to submit a manuscript, but did not fully understand the exact protocol. As my anxiety grew, agonizing questions consumed my mind. I wondered to myself; *What if I submit it wrong and they don't even want to read it? On the other hand, what if they think, "Who does this lady thinks she is? She can't write!"*

The night before leaving for Colorado, I sat upstairs in my loft crying. I put my hands on the manuscript and prayed, "God, forgive me if I have let You down, and please help me. I don't have a clue what to do or how to do it. Dear Lord, I need Your help in a big way!"

You see, my book was nowhere near ready to be submitted, and I could not understand why I struggled so. I promised God I'd have it ready to send off before we went to play in the snow, but that was not going to happen. On top of everything else, for weeks I had been asking (pleading) for guidance but not getting an answer. At one point I even yelled out, "Lord, I am listening, but I am not hearing anything!" I did not know it at the time, but I could not hear because I was too busy doing what I perceived to be the next logical step without having an understanding of what that meant. In my haste to meet my self-appointed agenda, I failed to realize something; I created this deadline, not God!

The next day we boarded the plane as I wrestled with feelings of confusion and depression. I prayed once again for God to give me peace as Bob lovingly reassured me the Lord had everything under control. I finally resigned myself to the fact time had gotten away from me, and that was that. Skiing is not cheap, and I needed to relax and enjoy our vacation. I slowly released the all-consuming feelings of anxiety and worry, and the spirit of joy gradually returned. As usual, Bob was right. I needed to calm down and trust God to help me figure out the next steps to take.

The plane steadily filled up, but the seat next to us remained empty. At the last minute a young woman with a baby hurried on board and I looked at Bob and said, "You know, she is going to sit next to us. I hope it's a good baby!" Bob smiled as she made her way down the aisle, and sure enough, she sat down next to me. Bob is shy and quiet, and I am just the opposite. I love meeting and getting to know strangers, so when we finally took off I decided to introduce myself.

The minute I told her my name she smiled and said, "My name is Donna, too, and my baby's name is Olivia." They were on their way to the 2002 Winter Olympics in Salt Lake City, Utah, to see her husband. He was a Sportscaster for NBC covering the Olympics, and she planned to surprise him for their anniversary.

As Donna and I continued getting to know one another, Bob leaned over and whispered in my ear, "Tell her about your book." I looked at him with a bewildered stare, because at that time we rarely told anyone about the book. I tried to be careful so that I did not appear conceited or as though I wanted to impress people. More than anything I desired to share my story as a testimony of God's power and mercy. I wanted to encourage others to step out in faith and dare to believe God for miracles in their own lives. When Bob asked me to tell Donna about the book, I knew he must have a reason so I went for it.

I briefly gave Donna my testimony and shared with her how I felt impressed to write my life's story to help others who are struggling. I explained how discouraged I had become because I could not find the time to get my manuscript off to Christian publishers before leaving for our ski trip. Before I could even finish my sentence she said, "It's a good thing you didn't, because you would have done it all wrong!" The next thing she said sent chill bumps all over us because we realized this had been a divine appointment strategically set up by God Himself.

It turned out Donna is a successful and notable author. She uses a pen name and writes fictional love stories filled with odd and unusual twist and turns. When she first decided to become a writer she spent thousands of dollars going to writer's conferences and conventions. She gathered all kinds of materials and information on how to submit a manuscript, including what to do and what not to do. She began telling me step by step how to proceed. She then offered advice on how to pursue someone to help me with the editing process before submitting my manuscript to Publishers. Bob and I were stunned and on the verge of tears. Donna had only one request, she asked me not to divulge her pen name when I shared my story.

Before long we arrived at our destination and found ourselves saying goodbye to our new friend and her beautiful baby. We could not thank Donna enough for the advice and help she so graciously gave us. As we walked away, Bob and I asked the Holy Spirit to continue bringing people into her life to water the seeds we had sown.

As I replayed the events in my mind, I thought about the prayer I prayed before leaving to go on our ski trip. "God, forgive me if I have let You down and please help me. I don't have a clue what to do or how to do it. Dear Lord, I need Your help in a big way!" I felt so ashamed for thinking He wasn't listening and unwilling to answer my prayer. At that moment I realized God's timing is always perfect and to stress over this book was ridiculous. I had been obedient to write it, even with all my reservations. Now I simply needed to trust the Father to direct my steps, and never forget that He is always working everything out for the good. His purposes and plans were going to be fulfilled and accomplished. With a renewed sense of peace, I finally calmed down as we set out to swoosh down the mountains.

On Wednesday we decided to find a local church in the area and attend their midweek service. Bob looked through the phone book and found one not too far away. We stopped for supper before church, and while we sat waiting for our food Bob looked at me and said, "Baby, wouldn't it be just like God to have someone like Donna was talking about who can help you with your book at this church we are going to?" As soon as he said those words I responded with, "No way. That would be crazy. There is one thing for sure. If that happened I would never have another doubt or question about whether God really wanted me to write this book!" Then I broke down and cried. Bob's faith stirred my spirit and caused me to feel convicted. You see, even with all the confirmations God continuously gave me, there were moments during those years I actually questioned the Lord and wondered if this was a God idea or Donna idea!

We finished our meal and headed off to church. Bob's words were like an echo in my ears as I quietly thought to myself: *Would You do that God? How incredible and miraculous it would be if You had someone in this church to help me!*

When we walked in the possibility of that happening quickly dwindled because there were only about ten adults counting us. We were greeted and ushered down to a table in the basement. The pastor explained that due to the recent growth in the youth group they stayed in the main auditorium on Wednesday nights, and the adults held their Bible study downstairs. That blessed us tremendously. We love to hear reports about youth groups growing and young people actually wanting to attend church!

The pastor opened in prayer, and then said something very interesting. He asked everyone to share a recent event where they knew God answered a specific prayer. The question was very precise. He asked for something *recent,* and Bob and I both knew that would be our encounter with Donna on the plane. I felt excited to share but reluctant. Once again, it meant telling others about my book and I did not want to come off as conceited or someone with a high opinion of themselves. I prayed for God to give me the wisdom to share my testimony with humility and gratitude.

Since we were new to the service, the Pastor decided to start with us. I took a deep breath and went for it. We introduced ourselves, and I briefly shared with them about my book. I told everyone how I felt before leaving home and shared how I prayed for God's help and guidance. I expressed my anxiety about not knowing how to proceed with the submission process, and finished with how beautifully God answered prayer by sending Donna!

Almost before I could finish the Pastor interrupted and said, "You need to get together with Jeanne Marie. She just published her first Christian fiction book."

With tears in our eyes, Bob and I just looked at one another. We were in awe on how God continued to move on our behalf, setting everything in motion.

Jeanne and her husband were both there and what happened next just about blew us away. She told me she had started a Christian editing service for new authors, and she would love to assist me with the editing of my book. How amazing is that! I settled it in my heart to never again doubt the words the Lord spoke to me about writing my testimony. He had a plan, and it would happen in *His time* and in *His way!*

For over a year, Jeanne Marie worked diligently to help me with the first edits of my manuscript. I will always be grateful for her insight and patience. It is wonderful to see how God is blessing her too. She currently has a number of Christian fiction books published and continues to mentor and help new, aspiring Christian writers!

Shortly after completing the first editing process, we felt the Lord calling us into full-time missions. My book would be put away for a season due to our many responsibilities, as we focused on radically changing our lives and heading off to missionary school.

After school, we participated in numerous mission outreaches to help front-line missionaries, along with ministry and building projects in Mexico. During those first few years, we also served Stateside as pastoral missionaries to young people who attended the missionary school.

We were about to make another transition because of a change in our mission's base, and I felt the Lord directing me back to my book. I decided to send out query letters to different publishing companies to see if anyone might be interested in my story. Months passed by, and I heard nothing. I knew how God had moved on our behalf in the past, so I was not concerned. I wanted it on His timeline, not mine!

Our base ended up merging with another mission's base from Colorado Springs, and we were required to go through more schooling. Once we completed the classroom phase, we went to India to serve with front-line missionaries. While working in India I received three e-mails from different publishers expressing interest in my story. All three of them somehow overlooked my previous query letters, and almost an entire year had passed since I sent them. God's hand remained steadfast and faithful in this situation.

By this time we were feeling a need to make a change in our lives, and we thought the sudden interest in my book may be the Lord guiding us in a new direction. In fact, before leaving for India we prayed for God to give us absolute clarity about leaving the organization we had been working with. Upon our return to the United States God answered our prayer so precisely it left no room for doubt.

The next phase of our lives found us making a permanent home in Colorado Springs and deciding which publisher to go with. Although we were at peace with the direction our lives had taken, our hearts were burdened about leaving full-time missions because of the family God had given us through our work. Many of our kids were missionaries, and we truly anguished over thoughts of not seeing them or being an active part of their lives. They needed us, and we needed them even more! No matter what, they always had a place to call home.

We did not have to worry long, because God orchestrated a beautiful plan to keep our family together. From the time we returned to the States and found a place to live in Colorado Springs, our home stayed filled with young people. In fact, for the first six months of settling into our new life, we did not spend one night alone without two or more of the kids home. We were overjoyed with how the Lord answered our prayers. Our God is an awesome God!

To this day, our home is like a revolving door. The many young people the Lord has given us keep our lives busy, fun, and exciting. We are so grateful for how God took care (and continues to take care) of every little detail. You see, *He is faithful, He is true, He is just, and He is beautiful!*

~The End~

Truth

It took a long time before *Falling into Faith* became a published, tangible reality. In fact, five years passed before holding a published copy in my hands. There were times during the process it felt like an eternity! In 2009 another blessing occurred. My book won the National Indie Excellence Award (NIEA) in the autobiography division. God is amazing and so faithful!

For the devotion part of this chapter, I want to focus on why we struggle when we are waiting for God to manifest a dream or call He has placed in our hearts. To do this we will examine the life of Saul of Tarsus, who after a radical conversion became Paul, the Apostle. He once persecuted Christians and vehemently opposed the disciples of the Lord. He was considered the worst of the worst; however, God had a glorious redemption plan for his life. Take time to read Paul's conversion in Acts 9. It is an amazing example of God's ability and power to reach the hardest of hearts!

I can barely sit still when I read the book of Acts. It is awe inspiring how God intricately worked every detail out in Paul's life in order to get the Good News of Jesus Christ spread to other nations. Paul truly is one of my heroes from the New Testament.

Let us begin this journey in Acts 19. Paul is in Ephesus, and we will explore the power and fruit of his ministry along with his commitment to spread the Gospel. We will also look at a very important statement Paul makes in verse 21. He expresses something that is on his heart. Something he must do!

"Paul entered the synagogue and spoke boldly there for three months, arguing persuasively about the Kingdom of God. But some of them became obstinate; they refused to believe and publicly maligned the Way. So Paul left them. He took the disciples with him and had discussions daily in the lecture hall of Tyrannus. This went on for two years, *so that all the Jews and Greeks who lived in the province of Asia heard the Word of the Lord. God did extraordinary miracles through Paul, so that even handkerchiefs and aprons that had touched him were taken to the sick, and their illnesses were cured and the evil spirits left them."* (Acts 19:8-12, NIV, emphasis added)

"In this way the word of the Lord spread widely and grew in power. After all this had happened, Paul decided to go to Jerusalem, passing through Macedonia and Achaia. 'After I have been there,' he said, *'I must visit Rome also.'"* (Acts 19:20-21, NIV, emphasis added)

God moved mightily through Paul's ministry; however, it was not an easy road. A lot happened to him because of his boldness and determination to spread the Word of God to both the Jews and Gentiles. He performed many miracles in the name of Jesus, but he also suffered persecution and prison. Through it all, Paul felt a burning desire to go to Rome.

What word or burning desire do you feel the Lord has given you about your future or present situation? When we decide to truly trust God with our lives we must come to an important understanding. Whatever comes our way will not keep us from our destination; instead, it is God's path and His direction toward that vision and purpose. If we continue to press into Father God and trust in His Word, then we will bring glory to His name and prepare the way for the miraculous to manifest in our lives and others!

As we go through this devotion, I want to challenge you to really look at Paul's life and the obstacles he faced when he chose to be obedient to God. Then look at how he responded to those difficulties. Ask yourself a tough question: "Will I seize the moment and take every opportunity to share the love of Jesus, or waste time complaining and questioning when my path takes an unexpected turn?"

Paul felt he must to go to Rome, but how would he get there, and when? This is where things got tricky. The road God took Paul down en route to Rome was hard and filled with twists and turns, but the Father had a purpose. He strategically planned every step of the journey so that His Word would reach as many people as possible, and also bring encouragement to the Believers!

The scriptures tell us the spirit compelled Paul to go to Jerusalem, although he knew prison and hardships were ahead. I believe getting to

Rome was never far from his mind, but being obedient to the Spirit of God consistently stayed his first priority. Read what Paul says about the journey that lay ahead.

"And now, compelled by the Spirit, I am going to Jerusalem, not knowing what will happen to me there. I only know that in every city the Holy Spirit warns me that prison and hardships are facing me. However, I consider my life worth nothing to me, if only I may finish the race and complete the task the Lord Jesus has given me—the task of testifying to the gospel of God's grace." (Acts 20:22-24, NIV)

Paul's farewell to the Ephesian elders proved to be bittersweet. He told them they would never see him again, yet he did not waver in his determination to go. He admonished them, "Keep watch over yourselves and all the flock the Holy Spirit has made you overseers." He went on to say, "Be Shepherds of the church of God, which He bought with His own blood."

After a time of prayer, they wept and embraced Paul as they accompanied him to the ship waiting to take their brother far away. The last verse of chapter 20 tells us they were grieved the most by the thought of never seeing his face again. I can only imagine how they felt. The gospel carried a price, and they knew it all too well!

On the way to Jerusalem, Paul's voyage took him to Caesarea, where he crossed paths with a prophet named Agabus. The prophet took Paul's belt, tied his own hands and feet with it and said, "The Holy Spirit says, 'In this way the Jews of Jerusalem will bind the owner of this belt and will hand him over to the Gentiles.'" (Acts 21:11, NIV)

The people cried and begged Paul not to go to Jerusalem but he responded with this: "Why are you weeping and breaking my heart? I am ready not only to be bound, but also to die in Jerusalem for the name of the Lord Jesus." You see, Paul could not be persuaded to give up on his mission. He may not have understood the why or how, but he knew the One who called him! The scriptures go on to tell us when Paul arrived in Jerusalem he reported to the elders in detail the things God had done among the Gentiles through his ministry. When they heard the report, they all praised God!

Paul was a chosen vessel by the Lord to carry the message of Christ to everyone, not just to the Jews. Due to his unwavering determination this boldness eventually led to his arrest, thus fulfilling the prophecy. Let's read what happened at the time of his arrest.

"The whole city was aroused, and the people came running from all directions. Seizing Paul, they dragged him from the temple, and immediately the gates were shut. While they were trying to kill him, news reached the commander of the Roman troops that the whole city of Jerusalem was in an uproar. He at once took some officers and soldiers and ran down to the crowd. When the rioters saw the commander and his soldiers, they stopped beating Paul. The commander came up and arrested him and ordered him to be bound with two chains. Then he asked who he was and what he had done. Some in the crowd shouted one thing and some another, and since the commander could not get at the truth because of the uproar, he ordered that Paul be taken into the barracks." (Acts 21:30-34, NIV)

As you can see, this became a very tense situation. Yet, in the midst of the chaos Paul made a request. He asked for permission to speak, and the commander agreed. Paul began testifying and preaching which eventually caused another uproar. Just when he was about to receive another beating, Paul said something extremely important; "Is it legal for you to flog a Roman citizen who hasn't been found guilty?"

According to Roman law, Roman citizens were assured exclusion from all degrading forms of punishment. When Paul asked this question the centurion went to the commander and reported it. The commander came back to Paul and asked him if he truly was a Roman citizen. Paul said, "Yes," and then the commander became alarmed because he realized he had put Paul (a Roman citizen) in chains. Not good!

Between chapters 23 and 26 a lot happens that is both interesting and powerful. Once again, let me encourage you to take time and read the adventures of Paul and the people he witnessed to everywhere he went. The Lord stayed by his side faithfully working things out, and Paul never ceased spreading the news of the resurrection of Jesus Christ.

Paul continued to be imprisoned because of preaching and testifying, but in the midst of this desperate situation God spoke to him concerning Rome. Ah, Rome, the place Paul knew he must go to!

"The following night the Lord stood near Paul and said, 'Take courage! As you have testified about me in Jerusalem, so you must also testify in Rome.'" (Acts 23:11, NIV)

Fast forwarding to chapter 27, Paul requested to plead his case before Caesar. As a Roman citizen he had a right to make this request, and it is what finally gets him to Rome. He is handed over to a centurion named Julius, who belonged to the Imperial Regiment. They boarded a ship and set out for ports along the coast of the province of Asia. Destination, Rome!

Paul found favor with Julius, and the next day they landed at Sidon, and Julius allowed Paul to go see his friends so that they could provide for his needs. From there, they went back out to sea, but soon encountered hurricane-force winds and a raging storm. This journey turned into a terrifying experience as the ship took a violent battering from the storm. They ended up throwing the cargo overboard to lighten the ship as the winds continued raging around them. Everyone had gone a long time without food, and there seemed to be no hope of being saved or surviving. God sent an angel to Paul with a message, so he rallied everyone together and began encouraging the terrified and weary men.

"But now I urge you to keep up your courage, because not one of you will be lost; only the ship will be destroyed. Last night an angel of the God whose I am and whom I serve stood beside me and said, 'Do not be afraid, Paul. You must stand trial before Caesar; and God has graciously given you the lives of all who sail with you.' So keep up your courage men, for I have faith in God that it will happen just as he told me. Nevertheless, we must run aground on some island." (Acts 27:22-26, NIV)

The ship eventually struck a sandbar and ran aground. It literally fell apart, causing some to have to swim ashore while others held on to planks and pieces of the ship. But just as Paul said, everyone was saved and no one lost their life.

Once everyone landed safely on shore they discovered they were on the Island of Malta, and the scriptures tell us the Islanders were unusually kind to them. They even built a fire to welcome everyone because it was raining and cold. Then something happened!

"Paul gathered a pile of brushwood and, as he put it on the fire, a viper, driven out by the heat, fastened itself on his hand. When the islanders saw the snake hanging from his hand, they said to each other, 'This man must be a murderer; for though he escaped from the sea, justice has not allowed him to live.' But Paul shook the snake off into the fire and suffered no ill effects. The people expected him to swell up or suddenly fall dead, but after waiting a long time and seeing nothing unusual happen to him, they changed their minds and said he was a god." (Acts 28:3-6, NIV)

Right before their eyes an amazing miracle happened, opening the door for an incredible opportunity for Paul. Let's continue to read how God revealed Himself to the people on the island of Malta. The next part of this story excites my spirit every time I read it!

"There was an estate nearby that belonged to Publius, the chief official of the island. He welcomed us to his home and for three days entertained us hospitably. *His father was sick in bed, suffering from fever and dysentery. Paul went in to see him and, after prayer, placed his hands on him and healed him. When this happened, the rest of the sick on the island came and were cured.* They honored us in many ways and when we were ready to sail, they furnished us with the supplies we needed." (Acts 28:7-10, NIV, emphasis added)

Years earlier Paul felt he *must go to Rome*, but he encountered obstacle after obstacle and numerous detours. Thanks to one of those bumps in the road, miracles were performed and an entire island experienced Jesus in a real and powerful way. All of this happened because Paul stayed obedient and faithful to the things of God!

What I love about Paul was his ability to not wrestle and struggle against the unexpected; instead, he used every opportunity to spread the hope of Christ. Even if it meant enduring a terrifying hurricane in the middle of the sea and being bitten by a poisonous snake. He knew God had everything under control, therefore, he chose to stay focused on his mission to testify about Jesus everywhere he went!

There is no way of knowing what Paul was thinking, but as we read chapter after chapter and see the obstacles he faced and how he responded, I do not think he ever lost sight of the fact God was with him. Even though he endured beatings and prison, Paul never stopped preaching and testifying, persuading and praying. That is what I call perseverance!

What about Rome? Did he ever make it there? Yes! When he arrived, he continued preaching the gospel and persuading men to believe in Jesus.

So here are a few questions to meditate on:

1. While we are traveling the road to our dreams how do we respond to the detours, turns, and bumps along the journey?
2. Are we so intent on the end results, we fail to see the opportunities the Father is giving us along the way?

This is my prayer and heart's desire. I want to walk this journey hand in hand with God. I do not want to waste one opportunity to spread the love of Jesus to those who are hurting and in need due to tunnel vision. My focus cannot remain on where *I think I should be* or what *I think I should be doing.* I want to get the "I" out of the way so that Jesus can be in control of the where, when, and how! I want to boldly *shake off* the things that try to hinder and destroy and learn *not* to struggle when life takes an unexpected turn. There are a lot of "I's" in these statements, but the questions are important. We need to be resolute in our love walk between God and man to ensure our lives are reaching outward, not self-centeredly inward!

When I find myself struggling, I pray God lovingly reminds me to *keep my eyes and heart on the calling He has placed on my life.* Only then will I reach my full potential as the mouth, feet, and hands of Jesus Christ my Savior!

Chapter 22

Choosing to Forgive

"Bear with each other and forgive whatever grievances you may have against one another. Forgive as the Lord forgave you. And over all these virtues put on love, which binds them all together in perfect unity." (Colossians 3:13-14, NIV)

Scripture Focus

"For if you forgive men when they sin against you, your heavenly Father will also forgive you. But if you do not forgive men their sins, your Father will not forgive your sins." (Matthew 6:14-15, NIV)

"Be kind and compassionate to one another, forgiving each other, just as in Christ God forgave you." (Ephesians 4:32, NIV)

Angie's Story

By Someone We'll Call Angie

For the sake of confidentiality, we'll call me Angie. I grew up in a kind, close-knit family where we loved being together and shared an adventurous spirit. We were there for each other in every way as we laughed, cried, and prayed together. Coming from this kind of an environment gave me a feeling of being loved and wanted; therefore, when I married a man with a quick and unpredictable temper it was a shock to my entire system. I was ill prepared to handle the rages, and I automatically recoiled inside, wondering how someone who says he loves me could be so cruel with his words. My heart said, *People who love each other don't treat them in such a reckless manner.* However, my mind said, *I love this man, and with God's help I can handle it.*

I handled the verbal attacks by accepting responsibility for my part in causing my husband, whom I'll call Dwayne, to lose his temper, and I prayed for God to help me be the wife He called me to be. I naively expected Dwayne to take responsibility for his part, but that rarely happened.

During the first years of our marriage, we enjoyed great times together, and the rages were infrequent. We learned to sail, became certified SCUBA divers, and traveled a lot. For a while, life was grand, but we faced many challenges in our marriage, as the verbal attacks increased. Little by little, I began to build a wall of protection around my heart, emotionally shutting out Dwayne.

In 1988 our son, whom I'll call Nick, was born. As he grew and began to challenge his dad the verbal attacks turned to rage, not only toward me but also toward Nick. I attempted to address the issues with Dwayne, and how his behavior affected Nick, but this just resulted in more attacks. From his point of view, everything was my fault. As a result, my energy became focused on protecting Nick from his father.

I remember Nick in hysterics, scrambling under the table to get away from his dad's verbal and physical attacks. My attempts to protect Nick seemed futile. With every attack, Dwayne was shooting holes in Nick's heart that I knew would take a lifetime to heal. The wall around my heart began growing higher and wider, and eventually my heart grew cold. Yet I still prayed to be a Godly wife, although I no longer felt I knew what that meant or how to accomplish this task.

One summer we took a vacation, and it became our dream to purchase land in the mountains and build our retirement home. In 1998 we purchased 35 acres in a remote place and began to build the house that was supposed to be the home where we would spend the rest of our lives. The dream seemed to be coming true.

As we spent time building our home, we began meeting some of the people that lived in the area. Many of them were into eastern mystical religions, Reiki (a type of ancient healing involving gentle massage therapy and deep relaxation, healing by using the universal energy, New

Age). I later learned that one of the couples we became friends with practiced Wicca (a polytheistic Neo-Pagan nature religion inspired by various pre-Christian western European beliefs, whose central deity is a mother goddess and which includes the use of herbal magic and benign witchcraft).

Our first experience with Reiki happened when Dwayne injured his back and required surgery. The first surgery failed and actually made his back worse. The muscles around his spine grew very tight and knotted, so we took a massage class together thinking it would help. The class included a full-day session on Reiki, and at the time I had no clue what Reiki was about. As the session progressed, I quickly realized this was not of God and was not something I did not need to be a part of in any way. By the end of the session I thought that Dwayne felt the same.

At first our time spent in the mountains was wonderful and peaceful. However, as time passed and friendships developed, it appeared a flame of intrigue ignited in Dwayne, and he became more involved in Reiki. He has the type of personality that when he does something he jumps in with both feet, and so it was with Reiki. He became obsessed. It consumed his every thought and eventually led to channeling (the practice of professedly entering a meditative or trance-like state in order to convey messages from a spiritual guide).

As his obsession grew he began trying to convert people, including me, to his beliefs. The more I clung to Christ the angrier he became and the more frequent and intense his rages grew. The wall around my heart became impenetrable and cold, but I clung to what little love I still felt for Dwayne. I did not like the wall around my heart, and my marriage seemed out of control. I did not know what to do. I did know this one thing: I married for life, and so I cried out to God for a miracle.

Dwayne had planned to retire in a few years. The sale of our current home would pay off the house in the mountains, and we would be set for our retirement years. Until then, we took frequent trips to the mountain just to get away from the hectic life of the city.

In preparation for his retirement, I began searching for jobs in our new area so we could move to the state we loved and be closer to realizing our dream. I applied for a position there and was hired within a short time. He planned to move out as soon as he could transfer with his job. This turn of events began a difficult, heartbreaking, and yet the most rewarding part of my journey with God. It taught me how to forgive not only Dwayne but also myself.

I remember unpacking the boxes in our new home and feeling more peace and contentment than I had felt in a long time. As I was cleaning the kitchen one day and feeling immense joy, out of the blue God spoke to my heart saying, "This is where I brought you; this is where I want you, but it is going to be difficult." Even though I did not want to admit it, I had a sinking feeling the difficult times had to do with my marriage.

The peace I felt was in stark contrast to the constant tension, and it seemed unnerving. I somehow knew the peace came from his being in our old house and me in the new. I began to experience guilt because I should want him with me. I failed to recognize how long I had lived in survival mode until the source of the tension no longer surrounded me on a daily basis.

Dwayne came out about every other weekend. At first I looked forward to his coming, until I realized when he came he brought the tension with him. As the time approached for his visits, I began experiencing anxiety attacks, and the peace I once felt disappeared as soon as he arrived. Sometimes I felt as if my insides were vibrating, and I wanted to jump out of my skin. Other times I felt like a huge boulder sat on my chest, and I longed to just yank it off!

During his visits, he began to pressuring me to study and learn about Reiki. He constantly talked about the people he met with the sessions he attended at a church that did not focus on Jesus Christ. He even started attending this church on a regular basis and became good friends with a counselor there. It seemed without me or Nick around he felt free to get heavily involved in Reiki, and his commitment increased. His anger toward me also grew because of my unwillingness to accept his beliefs. I learned later that the people he spent time with were counseling him to find someone with similar beliefs and leave our marriage behind. This did not help the situation.

On one particularly memorable visit, he asked me to go for a drive with him. I knew that this was not a good thing, because we had taken these drives before. He always spent the entire time talking about Reiki and how powerful it was, expressing how good it made him feel and the joy it brought him to heal others. Finally, he told me he sensed the more he talked and pressured me to accept his beliefs the more distant I became. He then said, "If you cannot accept and embrace Reiki the marriage is over!"

I could not believe what I was hearing. I told Dwayne, "You are asking me to choose between you and God." I knew God must be first in my life, and I determined to stand firm, knowing He would provide the strength I needed to walk through this situation.

Dwayne did not believe Christ is God, the Bible is the Word of God, or that Jesus Christ is the only way. He began challenging me to show him scripture where Reiki or energy healing was wrong. As I showed him the verses that warn us against conforming to the philosophical beliefs and wisdom of this world, and scriptures that tell us we must believe in Jesus, the Son of God or we will not have life, he grew angry. I showed him Nick 7:15-23, where Jesus specifically states that there will be those who come in "sheep's clothing" saying they prophesied, cast demons out, and performed miracles in Jesus' name, and He responded that He never knew them. At that moment he felt I thought he was evil. I did my best to convince him I did not believe he was evil; however, what he chose to be involved in was evil.

I knew I was in the middle of a spiritual battle, and I used the time he and I spent apart to renew and strengthen my relationship with the Lord. God also gave me a wonderful spiritual family to help me through this difficult time. They were there for me in every way as they walked, prayed, and cried with me.

During the Fall season after Nick and I moved to our new home, we spent a week in the mountains. Toward the end of the week, Dwayne became very angry with Nick. The verbal abuse escalated to pushing and knocking Nick down and ended with Nick running out of the house. I ran after him, and when I found him he said, "Next time this happens, I will defend myself." We returned to town early, and Dwayne left immediately to go back to the old community. Before leaving, he told me for the second time, "If you cannot accept and embrace my beliefs then our marriage is over!"

During one of my daily devotions, I read 2 Chronicles 20:15-17. These scriptures tell us how the enemy surrounded Jehoshaphat, and this frightened him, so he gathered everyone together and cried out to God. After they spent time in prayer and fasting, God provided the following response:

"Listen, King Jehoshaphat and all who live in Judah and Jerusalem! This is what the Lord says to you: 'Do not be afraid or discouraged because of this vast army. For the battle is not yours, but God's. Tomorrow march down against them. They will be climbing up by the Pass of Ziz, and you will find them at the end of the gorge in the Desert of Jeruel. You will not have to fight this battle. Take up your positions; stand firm and see the deliverance the Lord will give you, O Judah and Jerusalem. Do not be afraid; do not be discouraged. Go out to face them tomorrow, and the Lord will be with you." (2 Chronicles 20:15-17 NIV)

God again encouraged and spoke to my heart. He confirmed this situation was more than I could handle, and it was His battle. I did the best and only thing I knew to do; I prayed for protection for Nick and me and determined to hold on for the rough ride ahead.

In March the three of us were planning to go see *The Passion of the Christ*, and I prayed that God would use this movie to touch his heart. Teenagers can be challenging at times, and this turned out to be one of those days that resulted in a conflict between father and son. As the conflict heightened, Nick felt threatened by his father and took measures to defend himself. I do not think I have ever been more frightened in my life, and I thank God that the situation finally resolved without injury or worse.

Dwayne began telling me how everything that happened was my fault, and his talking soon escalated into a screaming rage. Unknown to me (but not to Dwayne), Nick had come down and sat at the bottom of the steps. Nick did this in an effort to protect me if necessary, and it broke my heart that he felt he needed to protect his mother from his very own father. At that moment, I let go of the love I had so desperately clung to. The love simply disappeared, and I felt nothing. Dwayne packed up and left, and Nick and I went to see *The Passion of the Christ*.

I did not hear from Dwayne for several weeks, and when I did, it was to communicate with Nick. Nick refused to have anything to do with his father for several months. He would not talk about the incident and refused to talk to a counselor. I knew he needed to deal with his anger and mend his relationship with his dad.

In the past, Dwayne had always stated counselors were people trying to solve their own problems, and he did not want anything to do with them; however, when I finally spoke with him a few months later he surprised me by saying he would go see a counselor with me. I made an appointment, and for the first few weeks went alone. He ended up only going to one session, and although I said very little, he worked himself up into such a frenzy it ended with him in the counselor's face, screaming. He then turned to me and asked what he could change to make the marriage work.

I responded, "For starters you can change the behavior you just displayed."

He replied, "That will never happen," then he wished me well and left.

When I received the divorce papers I thought, *Dwayne's been out of my life for a while; this will just be another day,* but it wasn't. In fact, I felt like something inside me died. I did not cry. I felt nothing—just empty and dry.

I told my counselor I wanted to walk through a door and see the sun shining, and feel like all would be well with the world and my life.

He responded with, "The process of healing is just as important as the healing itself. Relax and enjoy the journey."

But I did not know how to relax and enjoy anything at this point. Everything sounded and felt painful. I simply could not handle any more pain.

Life seemed to go in slow motion, and although it felt like an eternity, it had really only been about a month when I experienced my first turning point and began to heal. Our youth pastor spoke on Sunday morning about sacrifices that come from the heart and cost us something. At the end of the service he invited people to come forward and spend some time in prayer. People were flooding down to the altar, but I just stood there and prayed, *God, I took a stand for You, and it cost me my marriage."*

Softly, God spoke back to me and gently said, "Your sacrifice is pleasing to Me."

I cried for the first time since the divorce, and the cleansing tears came down like a flood.

I really did not want to forgive and did not feel that Dwayne deserved forgiveness, but I knew I had to be obedient to God. My heart tried its best to be sincere, as I told him, "I forgive you." I soon learned that I would have to repeat that statement of faith many times in the days ahead.

I prayed and asked God to help me break down the wall and turn my heart of stone to a heart of flesh. Little by little, the wall came down. Every time I forgave I would think, *Okay, now I can move on with my life,* then something would happen and my thoughts changed to; *Well, maybe not.* But each time a chunk broke away as God continued showing me the next thing I needed to forgive. The more I chose to forgive, the softer my heart became. As I grew stronger God began showing me where I failed and that I too needed forgiveness. He showed me that I built the wall because I did not trust Him and did not leave the battle for Him to fight.

I remember one particular time I began having anxiety attacks again, and I could not understand why. I thought I had come such a long way. I tried to ignore the attacks and just move on with my life, but the more I ignored them the worse they got. I thought I was about to have a nervous breakdown. God finally let me see the root of the problem. An individual I worked with had personality traits similar to Dwayne's and being around this person triggered my anxiety. In fact, at work I referred to him as "the bulldozer." I decided to go to management and ask for a transfer to another position where I did not have to deal with him; however, that was not God's solution. My supervisor informed me, "You are too valuable where you are, and you are needed here." Under normal circumstances I would have considered that a compliment and a good thing, but not this time.

A few weeks later a wonderful friend filled in for the pastor during a Wednesday night service, and she gave a lesson on prayer. In one of her points she stated, "When we pray we should not have any unforgiveness in our hearts."

God tapped on my heart and said, "You have not really forgiven him." Immediately I felt consumed with emotion and realized I still harbored resentment in my heart. This time I prayed a little differently. I asked God to forgive me for the unforgiveness in my own heart and asked Him to help me completely let go of anything I harbored against Dwayne. At that moment, the anxiety I had been experiencing just melted away. I suddenly felt free and rescued from both myself and the past.

As for Nick, he had a difficult time dealing with his anger, but God continued to work in his life. For a while he ran around with the wrong crowd. His grades dropped, and he began getting into trouble at school. For the first time in a long time, Dwayne and I worked together and decided that Nick needed to be rescued from his current environment. We made the decision to send him to a religious-based military school. He was adopted (watched and mentored) by the chaplain. That, in itself, proved to be an answer to prayer.

At first, Nick hated it there, and I would get heart-wrenching letters begging me to bring him home. Gradually he made friends and became involved in the school. Before long, they placed him in charge of the new boys. The commandant seemed very impressed with Nick's leadership skills, stating he did not scream and holler at the new boys like the others. Instead, he earned their respect by being patient and working with them as they adjusted and became oriented to the school.

As a senior, Nick was given one of the top positions at school and promoted from a noncommissioned officer to a commissioned officer: assigned as the company commander for Charlie Company. Due to his outstanding work with the new boys Nick also received the "Unsung Hero" award from the city.

Nick and I have come a long way, and we can see God's love and protection as we continue to be lifted up in prayer by many people. Every day is a work in progress, but God never fails to prove Himself faithful.

Letting go of unforgiveness changes everything; it brings freedom and a future full of hope. We are blessed! I now have a fresh outlook on life and a renewed sense of trust in my Father God. I know that He will never leave or forsake me, and His plans for my entire family are good and full of promise. Although I am often uncertain of what tomorrow holds, I have personally made a choice to embrace hope and not let go!

~The End—*And* the Beginning! ~

Truth

Abuse of any kind can be a difficult thing to overcome and forgiving the abuser is often unthinkable, but for the Believer there is no other option. Within our own finite reasoning and understanding, we do not possess the power and ability to forgive those who wound and abuse; however, *through Christ and His strength we can do all things!* The fact is, choosing to forgive supernaturally empowers us and breaks the prison chains caused by unforgiveness and bitterness. It brings freedom and health along with liberty to our spirit, mind, and body.

In my autobiography I went into detail about what forgiveness is and what it is not. The following is an excerpt from *Falling into Faith*, Chapter 14, "Church, Hypocrites, and Forgiveness."

"Regardless of the sin or situation, the scripture is clear. If we do not forgive, we will not be forgiven. Is this fair? Not always. Is it the right thing to do? Always. So why don't we? It boils down to a choice, and only you and God can answer this question.

*One thing to keep in mind is this, **forgiving is not forgetting or even trusting.** There are painful experiences many of us have endured that we will never forget; however, the power of forgiving causes anger and bitterness to flee. Memory can serve as a testimony of God's restoration power, as well as to help others who are suffering. When past hurts replay in your mind, offer praise to God for what He has brought you through, and with determination resist feelings of bitterness, condemnation, and anger.*

Depending on the situation, trusting the individual (or individuals) we have forgiven is not always an option or even wisdom, but with the help of the Holy Spirit and God's amazing grace, we can be overcomers and walk in love. Ask the Holy Spirit for help as you apply forgiveness and stay in the Word! It will sustain you and lead your feet down a path that promotes a growing, liberating, and healthy love walk."

My friend made the choice to forgive. And although this story was not easy for her to write, she forged ahead praying it would bring hope to others. With the help of the Holy Spirit, she began to understand the power of forgiveness and the importance of it in her *love walk* between God and man. The freedom she has experienced since choosing to forgive is evident in her life, and she wanted to share this testimony in an effort to minister to others who are hurting. I am very proud of my friend!

If you are struggling with unforgiveness and bitterness, choose today to let go and let God work in your heart. I, too, have walked through an abusive situation. Like my friend, I chose to forgive. After making that decision and seeking God for help, I experienced an incredible peace and my life dramatically changed for the better!

God is waiting for you to make the right choice so that He can do the same for you. No one can do it for us. We all must make our own choices. Your situation may be very painful, but you *do not* have to remain a victim. Instead, *you can be victorious!* In your weakness Jesus Christ will be your strength. His Word says, "My grace is sufficient for you, for My power is made perfect in weakness." (2 Corinthians 12:9, NIV)

Do not believe the enemy's lies for one more minute. *You can overcome,* and with God's help *you can be free* from the past! In fact, your testimony will serve as a message of hope and deliverance for others who are struggling with similar issues and challenges.

God loves you and has a good plan for your life. He is patiently waiting for you to call out to Him for help. He alone can give you the strength and courage needed to break free from the pain and bondage.

Sometimes it is wise to seek professional help. In fact, the Lord may have already placed a person in your life right now that can offer the guidance, encouragement, and prayer needed to take this leap of faith. Don't delay; reach out to a Pastor, Counselor, or Christian friend.

I will also be honored to pray and intercede on your behalf. Feels free to contact me through my website for prayer and spiritual counsel: http://www.donnawilcox.com. *Choose well, choose life!*

Chapter 23

Where Do I Go from Here?

"We live by faith, not by sight." (2 Corinthians 5:7 NIV)

Scripture Focus

"Now it is God who made us for this very purpose and has given us the Spirit as a deposit, guaranteeing what is to come." (2 Corinthians 5:5, NIV)

"But we have this treasure in jars of clay to show that this all-surpassing power is from God and not from us. We are hard pressed on every side, but not crushed; perplexed, but not in despair; persecuted, but not abandoned; struck down, but not destroyed." (2 Corinthians 4:7-9, NIV)

Faith in Action

By Elaine Wilson

My son John was killed on January 16, 2006, which put me in a state of shock. In the midst of trying to adjust to losing him, I was told on April 25, 2006, that I had breast cancer. It did not surprise me, because over the previous few months all the signs had been there; however, I was told they were only cysts, and I did not need to worry. Although I am not a doctor, I truly felt the stress from my son's death was the reason the cyst turned into cancer.

With this diagnosis of cancer I wondered; *Where do I go from here?* I told my immediate family but assured them I would be okay. I shed a few tears, but not once did I worry that I would not be healed. For fear of people bringing negative comments to me, I chose not to spread the news all over the community. I did tell my Church family, along with men and women of God who I knew would pray. Donna sent me healing scriptures to read every day. The power of God is released in our lives when we speak forth His Word in faith. I knew my healing was already in Heaven. I just needed to wait for it to manifest on Earth. Hallelujah! Satan tried to defeat me, but I wanted him to know his plans of death and destruction were not going to work.

I am blessed with the gift of faith, and therefore I had no doubt about God's power to heal. Once I experienced God's saving faith (Luke 5:20; Luke 7:50), I knew He could do anything *but* fail. With my faith intact I stood strong but could not understand the reason for this trial.

As a young Christian, Job was my favorite story in the Bible. In my early twenties, I remember explicitly asking the Lord to test me like He did Job, believing I would pass the test. We must be very careful about what we ask for! Of course, the Lord knew what was best for me, and He waited for *His* time to bring this to pass.

Dealing with cancer would not be easy. I knew that grieving over losing my son must be put on hold so that my faith could be put into action. I also knew something else very important; *I must walk by faith, not by sight* (2 Corinthians 5:7).

The oncologist wanted me to take four chemo treatments, and afterward he would do a PET scan to see if the cancer was gone. The treatments were hard, but God stayed faithful. I remember sitting in his office after the fourth treatment to discuss what to expect from my PET scan. I asked him, "What are the chances of the cancer being gone?"

He said, "Fifty, fifty, but don't get your hopes up."

I quickly replied, "I am already healed." He did not want me to be disappointed if the cancer was not gone, but I continued to assure him God had healed me. With absolute certainty, I spoke healing over my body with words of faith, *unwavering faith!* I thank the Lord for this precious gift.

"The word is near you; it is in your mouth, and in your heart, that is, the word of faith we are proclaiming." (Romans 10:8, NIV)

"If you point these things out to the brothers, you will be a good minister of Christ Jesus, brought up in the truths of the faith and of the good teaching that you have followed." (1 Timothy 4:6, NIV)

"But when he asks he must believe and not doubt, because he who doubts is like a wave of the sea, blown and tossed by the wind. That man should not think he will receive anything from the Lord; he is a double-minded man, unstable in all he does." (James 1:6-8, NIV)

A few weeks after the scan I went to the doctor. When he walked into the office he said, "Your cancer is gone, and you are normal." I already knew this in my heart, but I praised the Lord for confirmation. The doctor admitted that I was an exception to the rule, and he could not believe the report! Even with these results, he wanted to send me to a surgeon and schedule a mastectomy. I knew from the beginning that this procedure would take place as a precautionary measure. The surgeon appeared just as surprised as my cancer doctor with the results of the scan. He scheduled surgery for August 24, 2006, and it was a success. I only spent two days in the hospital before going home.

Throughout the treatments and surgery I still did not understand the reason for my illness. I knew my faith was strong, so what could God be up to? I soon found out the answer to that question.

I live in a little town of about fifteen hundred people, and everyone knows everyone. One day while at the bank, the teller that helped me stated she heard I had cancer and said she had been praying for me. We were talking back and forth, and I heard the Spirit of the Lord say, "Elaine, this illness isn't for you, but it's to help build someone else's faith." I wrote that statement on a piece of paper and put it in my journal when I arrived home, happy to finally know the reason for my illness.

I remember calling Donna one day to ask her if she thought I was weird. Of course, she answered a resounding, "No!" You see, I never went into a deep depression because of the mastectomy. People did not understand why I didn't walk around sad and depressed, but I couldn't.

I did not feel I had anything to be sad about. Of course I wish it had not happened, but it did, and I refused to disappoint my God. He was using me as an example, and He supplied me with an abundant amount of comforting faith throughout this trial.

Donna walked the same road when she went through cancer, and she understood the peace and joy of the Lord I experienced in the midst of this situation. In fact, we both decided if we are weird we like it that way!

"Therefore, brothers, in all our distress and persecution we were encouraged about you because of your faith. *For now we really live, since you are standing firm in the Lord.*" (1 Thessalonians 3:7-8, NIV, emphasis added)

When I went back for my check-up I smiled to myself as the doctors flipped through the pages of my chart, back and forth, looking to see if maybe they made a mistake. They could not believe how exceptional and miraculous the results had been.

As another precautionary measure the oncologist recommended that I take four additional treatments. Wanting to be wise, I agreed. They also recommended radiation treatments, even though the doctor admitted he was not sure if I needed them. I did not feel they were necessary, but I also did not want to give Satan an open door.

Not long ago, a lady called asking me for help in walking through her illness. She said she could not believe how much faith I had, and she wanted her faith to increase. Immediately my heart filled with joy, because I realized something important: *this is a person that needed to see faith in action!* I told her to call me anytime, day or night, assuring her it is all in God's plan, and her faith would increase. I asked her to read Luke 17:5 and 2 Corinthians 10:15, and to pray in the Spirit. She did not understand what that meant, so I went through the scriptures with her and prayed for God to give her an understanding.

As I write this, it is January of 2007. My son left this earth a year ago, and I can now grieve his passing. Because of my faith, God has delivered me from my sickness and given me the grace to stand firm in the face of great tribulation and adversity. I am thankful!

The Word says, "And without faith it is impossible to please God, because anyone who comes to Him must believe that He exists and that He rewards those who earnestly seek Him." (Hebrews 11:6, NIV) You see, it's all about faith: little *faith*, great *faith*, saving *faith*, healing *faith*, increasing *faith*, word of *faith*, joyous *faith*, steadfast *faith*, working *faith*, patient *faith*, lacking *faith*, tired *faith*, growing *faith*, kept *faith*, sound *faith*, effective *faith*, unwavering *faith*, praying *faith*, tried *faith*, victorious *faith*, holy *faith*. Whatever your faith, pray for it to increase in wisdom, love, and power!

~The End~

Truth

Elaine Wilson is a strong woman of God and a precious friend. We first met at the call center in Fort Walton Beach, Florida, and she was my boss for a brief period of time before the center closed. Having a strong Christian supervisor who loves God's Word and stands strong in her faith is a huge blessing. In fact, because of her faith Elaine had a nickname, "Evangelist Wilson!"

When Bob and I went into missions, Elaine supported our work with prayer and finances. Throughout the pages of this book are stories from a number of dear friends God gave us during my time at the call center. They selflessly and generously sowed into our mission's work, and we are thankful for their love, support, and friendship.

When Elaine called and told me about her diagnosis of cancer, a wave of panic went through my entire body. Immediately following the panic something strange happened; I felt a stirring of excitement in my spirit. Before you think I have gone off the deep end, let me explain. Elaine is not someone the enemy wants to mess with. She is strong in her convictions and quick to testify of God's goodness and power. This is how Elaine got her well-deserved nickname!

I knew in my heart we were going to see victory, and I also knew Elaine would not be quiet about God's amazing ability to heal and restore. But my heart still ached and grieved for her. She had already walked through so much with the passing of her son, and so many other obstacles she bravely faced through the years. Any normal person might have collapsed under the pressure, but not Elaine. Her faith would not be shaken, and I praise God for the example she set for so many people during this time of trial and tribulation.

When someone contacts me with a prayer request, my first response is always the same. "What does God's Word say?" You see, I learned a long time ago the importance of using the Word of God to defeat the enemy and break the bondage and lies of Satan. If someone says you are sick, learn to come against that curse with scriptures of healing. If you are in debt, pray scriptures of wisdom over your life and put them into practice. If you are depressed, the Bible is full of scriptures which offer healing and restoration from emotional and psychological challenges. It is a matter of choice, and what you choose to believe will determine the end result: victory or defeat!

I realize life can render many tough blows. But God is good and His plans for His children are good, and that will never change! We must purpose in our hearts not to give up or give in to defeat and despair. There are hard situations all around, but there is also victory to be found when we choose to look for the answers in God and His Holy Word.

I love Joyce Meyer's book *Battlefield of the Mind.* If you struggle with negativity and a defeatist attitude, I highly recommend this book. With the help of the Holy Spirit and the Word of God firmly planted in your heart, you *can* live an overcoming life in spite of the obstacles in your path. They can simply become huge stepping stones toward a growing faith and closer relationship with God.

What will you choose to do with the rest of your life? Will you choose to believe in a God who loves you and is willing to carry you through to victory? Or will you choose to walk in defeat and let the weight of the world with all its pain imprison you to the point of despair and hopelessness? It is your decision. You have read this often throughout my book: *choose well; choose life!*

Chapter 24

It's a Faith Thing!

"God is our refuge and strength, a very present help in trouble. Therefore, we will not fear, though the earth be removed, and though the mountains be carried into the midst of the sea." (Psalm 46:1-2, KJV)

Scripture Focus

"We are troubled on every side, yet not distressed; we are perplexed, but not in despair; Persecuted, but not forsaken; cast down, but not destroyed." (2 Corinthians 4:8-9, KJV)

"And the Lord shall help them, and deliver them; He shall deliver them from the wicked, and save them, because they trust in Him." (Psalm 37:40, KJV)

"For I the Lord thy God will hold thy right hand, saying unto thee, Fear not; I will help thee." (Isaiah 41:13, KJV)

"I, even I, am He who comforts you. Who are you that you fear mortal men, the sons of men, who are but grass, that you forget the Lord your Maker, who stretched out the heavens and laid the foundations of the earth?" (Isaiah 51:12-13, NIV)

The Big Picture

By *Sherrie Dewana Johnson*

Donna Wilcox has been a friend of mine for several years, and I cannot express the impact she has had on my life. Her life has been an example for many, and her teaching on faith encourages the very weakest to be strong.

When she asked me to write my testimony I could not help but think about the people who say to me, "I want to be like you, and I want to be a director of a large ministry like you are. I want what you have." All I can do is look them right in the eyes and say, "Do you *really* know what you are asking for? Are you *really* ready for that kind of sacrifice?" Having said that, allow me to share my testimony with you.

Everything was great, and life seemed to be perfect. My husband, Ronnie, had chosen to leave his military career, and we traveled the world enjoying many great adventures. We settled back home close to family, and we both had awesome Civil Service positions. I was a supervisor in Civilian Personnel, where I had been employed with Civil Service for over seventeen years. My job was one of the highest paid administrative supervisory positions in the organization. We have two beautiful children and enjoyed a lovely home in Florida by Lake Lorraine on the Shalimar Pointe Golf Course. Everything was just the way we wanted it. Then suddenly our lives drastically changed!

I received an unexpected and devastating call at work. My mother, who I talked with every day, had been involved in a terrible wreck. She was a transportation supervisor for the county school system and had gone that morning to give driving tests to bus drivers in the north end of the county. She locked her keys in the car and called my dad to bring her a spare key. On the way back, a semi-truck struck her head on—splitting the car into two pieces. My dad was following her and witnessed the accident. He could not believe the devastation. She told my dad she was dying and told him specific things to tell the children. Mom also told Dad things she wanted him to know as well. When I arrived at the hospital Mom had already been rushed to surgery, and I never got to talk to her. She later died in the emergency room.

I did not understand why God took her so early; she was only in her 50s and an active leader in the community and county, as well as the church. My mother and I were very close. That day I lost my mentor and best friend and my children lost their beloved MeMama. My son was very young and loved his MeMama dearly. He experienced tremendous problems coping with her death. He could not go to bed at night without sleeping next to me, holding my hand.

As if this was not bad enough, a couple of months later a trusted family member molested my daughter. The pain and suffering her and our family struggled with after this incident seemed more than we could bear. The difficulty grew even harder when my husband suffered a heart attack and underwent Open heart surgery with four bypasses. Ronnie suffered many complications, which resulted in eighteen hospitalizations in one year. He soon ran out of sick leave and ended up out of work with no pay.

Trouble continued to rain down on our family. Our son was attacked at school while boarding his bus for home. We were told he was a victim of gang violence, and he did not even know the name of his attacker. He had been brutally kicked and beat in the face to the point I did not even recognize my own son when I arrived at the emergency room. The emotional damage proved to be as painful as the physical pain he endured. He was out of school for over a year and would not leave the house. He closed all the blinds and curtains, refusing to let us open them. When he finally tried to go back to school, fear overcame him to the point he would start vomiting and could not stop. We ended up having to go get him and bring him home.

After seeing every member of my immediate family being attacked, I left my job of over seventeen years for a period of eighteen months to try and help our family cope. With both my husband and I out of work, we lost our beautiful home, car, furniture, and self-esteem.

Out of options, I finally returned to work, but then I suffered an attack. My supervisor (Chief of Personnel) changed five times in one year, and being in a key supervisory position this placed more and more demands on me. My workload increased tremendously and I had an additional three new sections under my supervision, causing me to work nights and weekends. I supervised and managed sections that affected over 5,000 employees. If Ronnie had to go to the hospital, my office brought the work to me there. Unable to withstand the pressure, I suffered an almost complete nervous breakdown and ended up on Workers Compensation. This drove me even further down into despair and severe depression. Unfortunately, I know what it means to plan your own suicide.

We were making only forty percent of what we use to bring home. No longer able to make ends meet, we lost our home for the second time and moved in with friends and family for brief periods of time. We were embarrassed and stressed to the max!

Ronnie continued to struggle with his health. He endured two more heart attacks, three more blockages, numerous heart procedures, and additional health problems. He also suffered with a severe hiatal hernia, which resulted in a constant cough. Due to this, Ronnie could not eat without throwing up.

I had been raised in a Christian home and always been involved in Church. I knew God existed and was still in control, but I had grown angry with Him due to the many attacks on my family. In spite of the devastation and pain, something deep inside my heart would not allow me to lose total faith in God. Feeling the need to draw closer to the Lord, Ronnie and I started volunteering our time to ministry by working in our church. Even though our lives were not perfect, as we stepped out in faith through this volunteer work, things began to change. We soon became the directors of ACTS (Active Christians Together in Service). This is a benevolence outreach, providing food, clothing, and other needs for the hungry and the elderly who are financially struggling or physically disabled.

In time, our pastor felt impressed for us to move into the church parsonage and run ACTS Ministry full time. You see, God had a good plan for our lives, and He began revealing it one piece at a time. He provided a home for us and allowed us to work in ministry, which was our heart's desire from the very beginning!

Over the past 13 years, God has placed key people in our lives. He brought a special friend in my life that has been a mentor and helped me overcome depression. You see, God even replaced what I lost as a result of my mother's death by giving me a mentor and a best friend.

By the grace of God, my daughter overcame the pain of being molested. She is married with three beautiful children. She received her degree, and both she and her husband are active in church and serving the Lord! My son overcame the emotional trauma from his grandmother's death and from being attacked and beaten. He is now married with two precious sons and is a certified minister. He and his wife are presently youth pastors at our church. He also serves as the Sectional Youth Representative for the West Florida District Assemblies of God, and Chaplain of the Navarre High School Football team. God is using him mightily! Even though my husband has been through many heart attacks and other serious, life-threatening health problems, the doctors are still unable to find permanent muscle damage to his heart. God is good!

Just when we thought things were perfect again, our lives took another drastic turn on March 3, 2004. The parsonage where we lived caught fire, and we lost everything. We lost our home for the third time. Our ministry seemed destroyed, and our lives were once again devastated. Not knowing what to do next, we decided to take one day at a time and step out in faith. We continued working ACTS from a small closet in the church, starting completely over from nothing. As we continued meeting the needs in our community and doing what God called us to do, what happened next took us completely by surprise!

After eleven years of faithfully working in the ministry, the windows of heaven seemed to open up and rain down on us. The needs continued to pour in, as ACTS grew beyond our expectations. Already busy from the rapid growth, hurricanes began pounding the coastline and Florida Panhandle. Then came Hurricane Ivan, and we were directly in its path. Our area suffered complete destruction along the coastline and severe damage to almost every home in the area. What happened next still amazes me! God set up divine appointments for our ministry. Connections were made, and trucks started pouring into ACTS. In the aftermath of Hurricanes Ivan, Dennis, and Katrina we were able to share in the spirit of giving and gave the message of hope and healing to literally thousands of people by providing semi truckloads of food and essential supplies to the suffering victims of the hurricanes. Semi-truck after semi-truck kept pouring in. Last year, ACTS gave over 4.6 million dollars' worth of supplies to the Gulf Coast victims. Our God is an awesome God!

We are also celebrating the construction of our new 5,000-square-foot "ACTS Dream Center." The Dream Center not only houses our benevolence outreach (which now is one of the largest Food Banks in Santa Rosa County), but also features "The Harbor Café" and 'The Harbor Book & Gift Store" for the entire community to enjoy!

When funds are available and through networking, ACTS offers assistance to the homeless and helps with health care, job opportunities, and other resources. For 11 years and counting, ACTS continues to brighten the holidays for thousands of people needing assistance with food and gifts. In addition to that, we also provide gifts and support during the holiday drive to the following agencies:

The Angel Tree Program
Hospice Care (terminally ill children)
Prison Fellowship Ministries (children whose parents are in prison)
The Foster Parent Association (Foster Care Children and Medically Disabled Foster Care Children)
Caring and Sharing
Grandparents Raising Grandchildren
Sickle Cell Anemia Foundation
Family Life Center
Lifeline Outreach
Family First Network

Throughout the year we work closely with organizations such as America's Heart Association, Toys for Tots, Operation Outreach, Interfaith Ministries, We Care Ministries, The Joseph Project, Bethesda Mission, Convoy of Hope, Waterfront Rescue Mission, Tri-County, The Salvation Army, Newark America, T.C. Trucking, Glory Company, and numerous other ministries along the Gulf Coast. Every day ACTS has families lined up to receive food boxes, as agencies over several different counties refer families to us for help.

We see miracle after miracle on a daily basis at ACTS Ministries. We can be completely out of funding, and someone will walk in with a check for the amount we need. We usually do not have enough turkeys to fulfill our Thanksgiving and Christmas Food Boxes, but then someone will walk in with loads of turkeys!

When God gave us the vision for a book and gift store to fund the ministry, he provided us with the resources to do it. For example, a gift shop in town that had been in business for fifty years closed down and blessed ACTS with their entire inventory. They literally handed over thousands of dollars' worth of top-of-the-line merchandise to the ministry, plus all of the shelving and cases we needed.

I know without a doubt God brought me and my family through all of these trials and struggles we have faced for such a time as this. I am a better person and a stronger leader because of what we have walked through. Now, I really can counsel and minister to people's needs. When someone comes in and says they have lost everything, they are facing health issues, they have been through a fire, or their children have been hurt; I can truly say, "I understand!" You see, God knew the *big picture* and what lay ahead. He allowed me to face these trials knowing I must walk through the valley before I could soar to the mountaintop!

~The End~

Truth

I wept and rejoiced as I read Sherrie's testimony! I cannot begin to imagine living through so much devastation and anguish. I love how she phrased the last sentence, "He allowed me to face these trials knowing I must walk through the valley before I could soar to the mountaintop!" It takes faith to walk through this kind of turmoil and make that statement. I am honored to know Sherrie and call her my friend and sister in Christ!

We all face trials and pain in our lives, but it is what we do with those challenges that brings about hope and victory, or despair and unending agony. It truly is a faith thing! Either we believe God is bigger than whatever life throws our way, or we don't. It is not what we say, but how we respond to our circumstances which ultimately tells the real story.

As Believers, it is important to keep our eyes on the One who suffered more than we can ever imagine. Jesus Christ endured the agony of the cross so that we may be redeemed, victorious, and have the promise of eternity in Heaven! He alone can see the big picture. *By faith,* we must choose to hold tight to God's Word and believe He is good. *By faith,* we steadfastly encourage and remind ourselves of an important fact; *our Heavenly Father is loving and faithful and He will victoriously deliver me!*

How is this possible when we are troubled on every side, with the storms of life crashing around us like a tidal wave? It may sound simple, but we do what Sherrie and Ronnie chose to do. *By faith,* we put our hands to the plow and become *servant driven* and *servant led.* What does this mean? Step away from "your troubles" and diligently do whatever your hands can find to do for others. When we stay wrapped up in our own problems, we create a breeding ground for additional pain and sorrow. It is emotionally, physically, and spiritually unhealthy. Reaching out to others allows us to keep things in a proper perspective because we begin looking outward, not constantly inward.

Sherrie and Ronnie learned this valuable lesson through running a volunteer ministry in their church. For you, it may be teaching children's church, a Sunday school class, or cleaning the church. Whatever it is, stay the course. Do not stop due to the pressures of life, and be patient! God will bless your obedience and carry you through to victory.

"Whatever you do, work at it with all your heart, as working for the Lord, not for men, since you know that you will receive an inheritance from the Lord as a reward. It is the Lord Christ you are serving. (Colossians 3:23-24, NIV)

I cannot help but reflect on those who have gone before us in the Bible. They suffered enormous pain for the cause of Christ, yet they rejoiced in victory and reaped bountiful benefits from their obedience. From Genesis to Revelation, God consistently brought forth blessings as a result of obedience and curses are reaped through disobedience.

Father God never wavers. He is just and good! Throughout His Word, those who continued to serve Him in love and faithfulness were blessed. Notice I did not say, *He blessed those who never made mistakes or faced weak moments.* They most definitely made mistakes, and they certainly faced weak moments! In spite of themselves, they kept falling into the arms of God and trusted Him to carry them through. Those who turned away in sin and disobedience were cursed, but those who stayed the course were blessed.

I do not want to be one who falls away and gives up. I desire to face life's challenges with the heart of a servant and a life that reflects faith, grace, and dignity. Always remembering, *God is my strength and my refuge.* Regardless of what life dishes out, He will bring me through victoriously. I am not alone; He is always with me. *You are not alone; He is always with you!*

Take time to read God's Word and truly examine the lives of those who have gone on before us. You will rejoice in the lives of Joseph, Moses, Abraham, David, Deborah, Ruth, Esther...and the list goes on! Take a moment to study why each one of these individuals were listed as *Heroes of Faith.* I pray it stirs your spirit and creates a hunger for a closer relationship with the Father. *By faith,* reach out to Him for He never ceases reaching out to us!

"*By faith* Abel offered God a better sacrifice than Cain did. *By faith* he was commended as a righteous man, when God spoke well of his offerings. And *by faith* he still speaks, even though he is dead. *By faith,* Enoch was taken from this life, so that he did not experience death; he could not be found, because God had taken him away. For before he was taken, he was commended as one who pleased God. *And without faith it is impossible to please God,* because anyone who comes to Him must believe that He exists and that He rewards those who earnestly seek Him." (Hebrews 11:4-6, NIV, emphasis added)

"*By faith* Noah....*By faith,* Abraham...and Sarah...*By faith* Isaac.... *By faith* Jacob...*By faith* Joseph...*By faith* Moses...*By faith* the walls of Jericho...*By faith* the prostitute Rahab...And what more shall I say? I do not have time to tell about Gideon, Barak, Samson, Jephthah, David, Samuel, and the prophets, who *through faith* conquered kingdoms, administered justice, and gained what was promised; who shut the mouths of lions, quenched the fury of the flames, and escaped the edge of the sword; *whose weaknesses were turned to strength*; and who became powerful in battle and routed foreign armies. Women received back their dead, raised to life again. Others were tortured and refused to be released, so that they might gain a better resurrection. Some faced jeers and flogging...others were chained and put in prison...they were stoned.... put to death by the sword...the world was not worthy of them...*These were all commended for their faith, yet none of them received what had been promised. God had planned something better for us so that only together with us would they be made perfect.*" (Hebrews 11:7-8, 11, 20-23, 30-39, NIV, emphasis added)

Chapter 25

Testimonies of Healing

"Nevertheless, I will bring health and healing to it; I will heal My people and will let them enjoy abundant peace and security." (Jeremiah 33:6, NIV)

Scripture Focus

"Heal me, O Lord, and I shall be healed; save me, and I shall be saved; for Thou art my praise." (Jeremiah 17:14, KJV)

"For I will restore health unto thee, and I will heal thee of thy wounds, saith the Lord. " (Jeremiah 30:17, KJV)

"Is any sick among you? Let him call for the elders of the church; and let them pray over him, anointing him with oil in the name of the Lord: And the prayer of faith shall save the sick, and the Lord shall raise him up; and if he have committed sins, they shall be forgiven him. Confess your faults one to another, and pray one for another, that ye may be healed. The effectual fervent prayer of a righteous man availeth much." (James 5:14-16, KJV)

"Who His own self bare our sins in His own body on the tree, that we, being dead to sins, should live unto righteousness: By whose stripes ye were healed." (1 Peter 2:24, KJV)

Trusting God

By Tracy and Maxine Grimes

My husband was watching the news on a local channel and they were talking about men getting PSA (prostate specific antigen) test and how important it was. He decided to go to the doctor and be tested. The results came back with disturbing news. His PSA was high, and they diagnosed him with prostate cancer. The doctor stated he needed surgery. Further testing revealed the cancer was aggressive and had spread outside of the prostate. We found this out in November, and they scheduled surgery in January.

When we heard the report we listened but somehow knew in our hearts God would take care of everything. For two months, we took communion at home every day. We knew the Word of God says, "By His stripes we are healed." We made a decision not to worry and put the matter in God's hands.

After surgery, the doctor said everything went perfectly, and he removed all of the cancer. He said that patients who trust God seems to do better than those that do not. He also said fear can cause cancer to spread even faster!

More than twelve years later, my husband is still cancer free. We praise Our Heavenly Father. He is so good to us.

No More Fever

By Tera Belle Hamilton

By the time I turned five years old I was small, sickly, and a very fussy eater (unlike today). I began suffering with chills and fever every day. The doctor said I had malaria, and back in the 1930s there was not a lot they could do for someone with this illness.

My family attended Kinston Assembly of God in Kinston, Alabama. Reverend O.C. Hickman was the pastor. He knew that I had been ill due to so many high fevers. One particular night at church while I lay on a pallet, the members were at the altar praying, and the pastor came over to me and prayed for God to heal my body. The next day I did not have fever or chills, and when we went back to church Pastor Hickman asked, "Has she had any more fevers?" Mother told him I had not had any more. The Lord instantly healed me the night the pastor prayed, and to this day the fevers never returned. The Lord is good!

The Tumor Is Gone!

By Dr. Donna Wilcox

A group from our mission's base traveled to a neighboring town to minister. After praise and worship, the pastor asked me to share my testimony of healing. As I began to speak, I felt a powerful moving of God within that small congregation. It brought to mind the scripture which says, "For where two or three are gathered together in my name, there am I in the middle of them." (Matthew 18:20, AKJV)

After testifying, I asked those who were sick or in need of prayer to come forward. Several lined up around the altar as our mission's team began to pray for each one. When I reached out to pray for a particular young lady, she looked up and asked for prayer but did not say why. I felt the Lord speak something specific and I leaned in and quietly shared it with her. She immediately began to shake and cry. I assured her the Lord had control of her situation and to look for a miracle. God wanted her to know first-hand the power of His Word; therefore, she must speak scriptures of healing and claim His truth over her situation. I wrapped my arms around this precious teenager and continued praying as she wept before God.

It is quite intimidating to share something you feel God has spoken to your heart. It truly is an act of faith. I have seen this abused so much in churches and mission's organizations, so I am extremely careful and always pray for Godly wisdom. I grew up hearing people say to others during prayer, "The Lord said this," and "the Lord said that." Unfortunately, many readily received those words and never sought God for confirmation. Sadly, the end result turned out differently than what they were told.

Yes, the Lord can and does speak through other people concerning our lives; however, we must ask ourselves two important questions:

1. Does it line up (agree) with scripture?
2. Have we sought God for confirmation ourselves?

We have a responsibility to hear from God ourselves. When I feel the Lord has spoken something to my heart concerning an individual, first I make sure it lines up with His Word. Next, I ask the Lord if this is something I am to intercede and pray about, or share with that person. If it is something I am to share, I begin with, "I want to tell you something God has put on my heart, but please take it to Him in prayer and ask for confirmation." Usually when this happens the Lord has already spoken to that individual, and what I tell them simply confirms what God has said.

I never want to assume at any time that I am not capable of making a mistake. After all, I am human and quite fallible; however, God is infallible and perfect in every way. He will bring clarity to our situation. The Father sent His Holy Spirit to guide us toward truth, and when we seek Him for confirmation, He will answer!

When we left church that day, I asked God to reveal the power of His Word in amazing ways throughout the congregation. A few days later I found out He did just that! The pastor called our house and asked if I remembered praying for a teenage girl at his church. I said "Yes" and asked if everything was okay. He started to cry and said the parents called him with some amazing news. This beautiful child had suffered with stomach problems for several months and had been diagnosed with a large tumor in her abdomen. When she came to church that morning, she asked God to heal her. After I prayed with her she told her parents, "God has healed me; the tumor is gone!"

Her parents said she started speaking healing scriptures over her body that Sunday and continued until the day they went to the doctor to discuss her upcoming surgery. She told the doctor she did not need surgery and asked him to take another x-ray. He did not see the need to do so, but he reluctantly agreed. When he came back in the room he happily exclaimed, "You are right, the tumor is gone!"

This young girl will never be the same. She has experienced firsthand the power of a Living God in a way that will stay with her as long as she lives. She can use this miracle as a testimony to encourage others to seek God concerning their situation, so they too can receive a miracle. When Jesus Christ does something amazing for us we must not keep quiet. We have a responsibility to testify! "And they overcame him because of the blood of the Lamb, and because of *the word of their testimony...*" (Revelation 12:11, AST, emphasis added).

If you feel as though your life lacks power and you are beat down, ask yourself an important question; "Am I daily testifying for Christ, and sharing His goodness with others in word and deed?" If the answer is "No," allow me to challenge you to make a change. Begin sharing with others what the Lord has done for you. I guarantee an amazing and powerful transformation will happen. The change will radically alter the course of your life, and serve as a testimony to others!

~The End~

Truth

I pray these stories have touched your heart and put a desire in your spirit to draw closer to the Lord. He longs for an intimate and genuine relationship with His people. Oh, how desperately we need to awaken the resurrection power of Jesus Christ that is within every Believer so our lives will reflect blessings, victory, and the heart of a servant toward our fellow man! Make a choice today to apply God's Word to your life, and become the hands, feet, and mouth, of Jesus Christ our Lord. Walk in love and remember, we are not promised tomorrow so make the most of today!

I want to close this chapter with another excerpt from my autobiography, *Falling into Faith.* It is undeniable proof God will sustain, heal, and bring to pass His purposes for our life. In this chapter I talk about the angel God sent to not only comfort me, but also offer a message of hope for a blessed future. At the time, I was nineteen years old and barely clinging to life as I lay in a hospital bed with tubes and needles everywhere.

Eighteen long years came and went before the promise God gave me in that hospital room began coming to fruition. So many times I wondered if I would ever have a day without pain or experience the joy of having a family of my own. God is faithful my friend and He is not slow concerning His promises. Hold on, stand firm, and trust in His timing.

"The Lord does not delay and is not tardy or slow about what He promises, according to some people's conception of slowness, but He is long-suffering (extraordinarily patient) toward you, not desiring that any should perish, but that all should turn to repentance." (2 Peter 3:9, AMP)

Keep this in mind as you read the following excerpt; I was a young lady, suffering with a disease that went misdiagnosed since childhood. Hospitals and doctors, along with surgeries and medicines were a regular part of my existence. Life as I knew it was not worth living, and I often wondered why God did not just take me on to Heaven. I am so thankful He saw the *BIG PICTURE,* and knew a lot of kids were in my future who needed "Mama Donna" and "Papa Bob" in their lives!

Excerpt from *Falling into Faith* Chapter 8, "Honeysuckle and Vanilla"

Overwrought with despair, all I could think about was another wasted year filled with hospitals and pain. Barely eighty pounds and looking like a walking skeleton, thoughts of never being able to have children consumed me.

I soon grew strong enough to go home, but I did not want to leave the hospital in a gown. Without anyone knowing, Dad decided to go shopping all by himself. He wanted to purchase something special for me to wear home. What he brought back caused quite a stir. It was a size one white jumpsuit, with "pit crew" and gas station names written across the pockets and sleeves, and a new pair of tennis shoes. No one could believe it! Robbie was the tomboy. I was the prissy one, but he beamed with excitement while everyone else chuckled. Not having the heart to say, "Daddy, what were you thinking?" I proudly wore it home, thankful to have such a loving father.

I left the hospital with some minor stomach pains, but the doctors assured me they would pass. By the time we arrived home, it seemed the pains intensified with each passing hour and throughout the night Mom had to change my gown several times due to waking up completely wet from sweat. The next day I ran a high temperature as the pain continued. My parents called the doctor, and he told them to bring me back to the hospital.

X-rays revealed adhesions throughout the abdomen wrapping around and blocking the intestines. This caused a serious bowel obstruction. Emergency surgery was done, removing over six feet of adhesions and intestines. This seemed hard to believe considering my weight and size. The small intestine is about twenty feet long, and the large intestine is about five feet long. The human body and all its intricate details is quite amazing. It makes me wonder how anyone can doubt there is a God.

After a few days and noted improvement, I returned home. Surely nothing else could go wrong. If only this had been true. While lying on the couch and visiting with a friend I smelled a terrible odor and noticed my gown was wet around the incision area. My friend panicked and ran to get Mom and Dad. They checked my stitches and to our horror my stomach had burst open. Dad called the doctor, advising him of the situation. He suspected infection and possibly gangrene. All the way back to the hospital I cried and screamed, "God, please let me die; I can't take any more!"

We arrived at the hospital with everyone in tears. My parents could not console me, and they were just as distraught. Only Jesus could deliver me out of this hell, but the only deliverance I wanted was death. Heaven held a much greater appeal than living one more minute on this earth.

As the surgeon entered the room I quickly informed him I was prepared to die and did not want another surgery. Taking my family out to the hallway, he advised them due to my state of mind and physical condition, putting me to sleep presented too many dangers. The doctors felt my only chance of making it through this ordeal meant doing the procedure with me fully awake. Although I faced a risk of going into shock, they *felt certain I would never wake up from anesthesia. My poor parents reluctantly agreed, and they proceeded without anesthetic.*

I don't remember a lot about surgery except feeling intense pain and anger! Throughout the entire procedure, I pleaded with God to take me home. Tubes were everywhere, up the nose and down the throat with needles in my arms, neck, and chest. The tubes were pumping poison and infection out of my body and into large tanks that looked like scuba diving equipment. A large needle was stitched from the neck into my chest, administering some kind of medication to the heart. I can still recall how helpless I felt. If only I remembered what David said, "When I am afraid, I will trust in You. In God, whose Word I praise, in God I trust; I will not be afraid, what can mortal man do to me?" (Psalm 56:3-4 NIV).

As I was in and out of consciousness, the doctors prepared everyone for the worst. At one point, I remember waking up and seeing nothing but sad faces. Daddy looked as though he was a million miles away.

During times of consciousness, I could barely talk, and if I did, the tubing crimped in my stomach, setting off all the alarms. To fix the tube the nurses had to bring it up, and then reinsert it back down the throat and stomach. The pain was excruciating. During this procedure, the needle in my chest had to stay completely still and in place. Mom often assisted the nurses by holding the needle and comforting me as they worked to fix the tube. There was a shortage of nurses during this time, but with great compassion everyone worked tirelessly to keep me alive, whether I wanted them to or not.

An amazing thing happened after one of these agonizing tube episodes. As pain gripped my body and I once again prayed to die, a beautiful figure appeared by the bed with a bright light shining all around. I immediately sensed this was an angel. An indescribable peace flooded my weary heart. The angel picked me up in its arms as we waded through what looked like a sea of infection and pollution. With a soothing calm the angel rebuked me for praying to die. It stated: "Many children will pass through your arms and be blessed; there is still a work for you to do. You will not leave this earth until your work is complete." My spirit stirred with humble appreciation and a shot of much needed faith. In spite of my angry and bitter heart, God still loved me enough to send a guardian angel to bring comfort and hope.

During times of unconsciousness, I could hear people talking. Nurses speculated about how long I would live or if I'd make it through the night. Through it all, the angel stayed with me for a total of twenty-one days. In moments of discouragement when I wanted Mother, it spoke in a calm and soothing motherly voice. In times of fear and panic when I wanted Dad, it spoke in a strong and firm fatherly voice. Whatever I needed the angel became, whether it was a mother's gentle touch or a father's firm assurance.

The angel brought something else very special to the room. The entire time it stayed with me I only smelled a lovely fragrance of honeysuckle and vanilla. The smell of infection, gangrene, and medication disappeared. Every day for three weeks it carried me in its arms, speaking scriptures of hope, blessings, and life:

"...never will I leave you; never will I forsake you."

"I can do all things through Christ which strengtheneth me."

"Being confident of this, that He who began a good work in you, will carry it on to completion until the day of Jesus Christ."

"...My grace is sufficient for you, for My power is made perfect in weakness..."

(Hebrews 13:5; Philippians 4:13; Philippians 1:5; 2 Corinthians 12:9)

The number of scriptures the angel spoke are too numerous to write. It still amazes me how loved I felt as the Word of God miraculously sustained me. Difficult obstacles lay ahead, but thanks to this heavenly visitation, I knew God still loved me.

Psalm 91 is evidence God sends His angels to watch over and protect His children. In fact, my angel did exactly what is written in verse eleven.

"For He will command His angels concerning you to guard you in all your ways; THEY WILL LIFT YOU UP IN THEIR HANDS, so that you will not strike your foot against a stone. You will tread upon the lion and the cobra; you will trample the great lion and serpent. Because he loves Me, say the Lord, I will rescue him; I will protect him, for he

acknowledges My name. He will call upon Me, and I will answer him; I will be with him in trouble, I will deliver him and honor him. With long life will I satisfy him and show him My salvation." (Psalm 91:11-16 NIV, emphasis added)

I pray this story encouraged your heart to hang onto God and take Him at His Word, for He alone has the power to manifest a miracle in your life. His plans for you are even greater than what you dare to dream or imagine. If you are not convinced, read this next scripture and ask the Holy Spirit to speak to your heart right now!

"Now to Him Who, by (in consequence of) the [action of His] power that is at work within us, *is able to [carry out His purpose and] do superabundantly, far over and above all that we [dare] ask or think infinitely beyond our highest prayers, desires, thoughts, hopes, or dreams."* (Ephesians 3:20, AMP, emphasis added)

As you pray and seek the Lord, it is vitally important to yield your life over to God's will and His timing. It doesn't mean you won't question Him or that you will never have moments of despair. Questions will arise and despair has a way of trying to overtake us; however, *true faith* stands firm. In spite of everything (and I mean everything) *true faith* will consistently choose God's Word and His truth!

No one but God knows when, where, or how your miracle will come. Even though I had to wait eighteen long years, with complete confidence I can tell you *the wait was worth every minute!* Surprised? Don't be. What I learned along the way and the relationship I found in Christ is worth more to me than any miracle, any amount of money, and absolutely all the pain and heartache I endured throughout the journey!

I pray this devotional has increased your faith in God and put a desire in your heart to seek after Him with stubborn determination. If you choose to follow Christ you will not regret it. The joy and peace that will flood your soul is indescribable, and your life will be a testimony to others of the love and mercies of this wonderful Father, Savior, Redeemer, and Friend.

If you are a Believer, stay the course. Your Father will never leave or forsake you, and His plans will be gloriously fulfilled in your life. Don't be afraid to dream, and dream big! Share the love of Christ with others every day. Live a life that is servant driven and remember the two greatest commandments Jesus gave us; *love God and love others!*

"One of the teachers of the law came and heard them debating. Noticing that Jesus had given them a good answer, he asked him, 'Of all the commandments, which is the most important?' 'The most important one,' answered Jesus, 'is this: "Hear, O Israel, the Lord our God, the Lord is one. *Love the Lord your God with all your heart and with all your soul and with all your mind and with all your strength." The second is this: "Love your neighbor as yourself." There is no commandment greater than these. '"* (Mark 12:28-31, NIV, emphasis added)